THE RIGHT WAY TO
PLAY CHESS

THE RIGHT WAY
TO
PLAY CHESS

David Pritchard

Revised and updated by Richard James

RIGHT WAY

Constable & Robinson Ltd
3 The Lanchesters
162 Fulham Palace Road
London W6 9ER
www.right-way.co.uk
www.constablerobinson.com

First published in the UK 1950

This new, completely revised and updated edition published by
Right Way, an imprint of Constable & Robinson, 2008

A copy of the British Library Cataloguing in Publication Data
is available from the British Library

ISBN: 978-0-7160-2199-5
Printed in Great Britain by Clays Ltd, St Ives plc

5 7 9 10 8 6

CONTENTS

INTRODUCTION

There has been much debate about the origins of chess but most authorities consider the Indian game of Chaturanga, for which documentary evidence exists from the early seventh century, to be its earliest precursor. The pieces for this game were essentially the same as for the modern game of chess: the king, the counsellor, which later became the queen, the chariot (rook), elephant (bishop), horse (knight) and footsoldiers (pawns). This game travelled east to the Islamic world, where chess flourished for more than 150 years from the late eighth century under the name of Shatranj. The game soon spread to Europe via invasions and trade routes, and by about 1000 it was well known throughout the continent. While some of the pieces (the king, rook and knight) were the same as we know them now, the other pieces had more limited moves. The pawn could only move one square forward, the piece we now know as the queen could only move one square diagonally and the equivalent of the bishop only two squares diagonally.

In about 1475 in Spain the game underwent a sudden and dramatic revolution. The queen and, to a lesser extent, the bishop, became much more powerful than previously, and the game was transformed from a rather slow and stately pastime to the exciting game we know today.

The mid nineteenth century saw tremendous advances in chess organization. Chess clubs were founded and tournaments at all levels organized. Developments in public, and later, private transport made matches between chess clubs possible and competitive chess available to everyone.

Chess received another boost in 1972 when the world championship match between Bobby Fischer and Boris Spassky made international headlines, mainly, it must be said, for reasons not directly connected with chess. Tournament entries and club membership increased dramatically and many parents wanted their children to learn chess. Although the boom proved to be something of a temporary phenomenon the effects are still felt today, more than 35 years later.

In the twenty-first century, chess faces a new set of challenges. The computer age has seen radical changes in the way people spend their leisure time, and this has impacted on chess, along with much else. Millions of people, doubtless more than at any other time in the game's history, now play chess, but at the same time chess clubs, at least in the United Kingdom, are finding it difficult to survive as chess can now be played readily at home, either against a purpose-built chess computer, or against chess software for a PC, or against human opposition using the Internet.

Chess software is now available, which, for the price of a ticket for the theatre or a football match, will play you at whatever level you choose – and at the top level these programs can beat the best players in the world. On the Internet, chess can be played in real time at any speed you choose against opponents from anywhere in the world, or by email or computer notification with several days for each move.

The increasing strength of chess software, along with the rapid dissemination of information by electronic means, has had an enormous effect on the nature of professional chess over the last couple of decades. Nowadays, the professional chess players have analysed the major opening variations twenty or thirty moves deep, and a new move played, say, in Siberia today will appear in your Inbox the next morning if you haven't been able to watch the game live over the Internet.

Chess was popularized in the old Soviet Union in the 1930s and, as a result of this, the majority of professionals still come from Russia and other Eastern European countries, although Asian countries such as India and China are developing into the new chess superpowers. For the Western Grandmaster, on the other hand, coming from a country with a higher standard of living, the safer option of a traditional career often proves more attractive than a life in chess.

But below the top players there are other chess professionals who make money out of media work, writing and teaching. In some parts of the country there is a considerable demand for professional chess tuition, mostly for children, and some who provide this service are gifted teachers who enjoy working with children, but are not necessarily themselves of master strength.

The other major change in chess since this book was first written has been the game's growth in popularity amongst children. Between the 1950s and 1970s chess was played mostly in secondary schools, but in the last thirty years chess has been very popular in primary schools. More than 70,000 children, mostly of primary school age, take part every year in the UK Chess Challenge, which is organized through school and other chess clubs. But this in itself presents another problem in that, while a few primary school pupils reach a very high standard, most make little progress and give up the game before moving to secondary school. There is also now a much wider range of activities open to young people as well as a greater level of academic pressure, so it is increasingly difficult to persuade teenagers to maintain their interest in chess.

In spite of all these changes, though, chess remains the same. The pieces are essentially the same as they have been for about 1400 years, and they move the same way as they have for more than 500 years. It is popular throughout the world, increasingly so in much of Asia, although it has yet to conquer Japan and Korea where they have their own versions of chess. It is a game without boundaries. It can be played and enjoyed by both young and old, regardless of sex, race or religion. Physical handicap is no barrier to success: there are many excellent blind players. Those who are housebound or live far from major centres of population can play by post or on the Internet. A game of chess can be as quick or as slow as you like. Many of those who enjoy Internet chess prefer 1-minute chess where each player has just sixty seconds to complete the whole game, so don't believe anyone who tells you chess is slow and boring. On the other hand, games played by post can last several years. The game of chess is a perfect balance between tactics and strategy and has an extraordinary inherent beauty. Look at the way the knight moves and you'll see what I mean. It has an extensive literature whose richness is unrivalled by any other pastime, and an endlessly fascinating history and heritage. Numerous studies have claimed that children who study chess gain considerable educational benefit from doing so, and it has also been shown that playing chess helps older people keep their brain active and staves off the onset of dementia.

   To be honest, chess isn't an easy game. If it was, there would be little point in playing it. It isn't a game for everyone, and any attempt to suggest that it is risks being counterproductive. Chess really doesn't benefit in the long term by being, in the current parlance, "dumbed down". At the same time, although you need to have a strong mathematical/logical and visual/spatial intelligence to play well, academic success is by no means essential for chess success. Of course, you might also choose to define success as how much you enjoy playing rather than how well you play, and, on that count, weaker players are often more "successful" than stronger players. Because it isn't an easy game, players, especially those starting out, need guidance to point them in the right direction. A vast amount of knowledge about the best way to play chess has been accumulated over the past 500 years, and, unless you tap into this information yourself you will stand little chance against someone who has done so. And that is where this book comes in.

The Right Way to Play Chess was written in 1950 by David Pritchard, a leading chess expert and teacher, who had continued to update the book through several editions. Since then it has continually been one of the bestselling chess books in the United Kingdom and has been recognized by two generations as one of the best guides for adult beginners on the market. David sadly died towards the end of 2005 and I was asked by the publishers, and with the blessing of his family, to prepare a new edition.

In this new edition I have rewritten some of the more topical sections taking the changes outlined earlier in the introduction into account. I have also computer checked all the analysis, amended the notation to bring it into line with current practice, added a topical game to Chapter 8 and made minor changes to the vocabulary and grammar to reflect contemporary usage.

At the request of the publishers, I have added a new chapter on teaching children to play, based on my 35 years' experience in chess education. In order to get the most out of playing at school, young children really need constructive help and support at home. If you have children yourself, please read this chapter, along with the rest of the book, before you start teaching them to play.

It has been a great pleasure to help bring this timeless classic to a new generation of readers. I hope you will gain as much enjoyment from reading it as I have from preparing this revised edition.

Richard James

1

HOW THE GAME IS PLAYED

The Game
The game of chess is played between two players on a board of sixty-four squares (8 x 8) alternately coloured light and dark (usually referred to as black and white).

Each player has at his command a force of sixteen pieces: one king, one queen, two rooks, two bishops, two knights and eight pawns. The opposing forces are of light and dark colours, and are referred to as White and Black.

Players move in turn, and the object of the game is to trap (checkmate) the opposing king.

Each chess piece is governed by its own rules of movement and is now examined separately.

The King ♔♚
The king moves one square in any direction (diagram 1) but, since he takes seven moves to cross the board, he is a comparatively weak piece. However, the importance of the king is evident from the second to last paragraph – his loss entails the loss of the game.

The king may not, therefore, be moved onto a square attacked by an opposing piece. If the king is attacked (i.e. if he is *threatened with capture* on the next move), he is said to be "in check", and the opponent may, but is not obliged to, say "check" when making the move that attacks the king.

The player whose king is threatened *must immediately move out of check*. There are three ways of doing this:

1. By moving the king onto a square not attacked by an enemy piece.
2. By capturing the checking piece, either with the king or with another piece.
3. By interposing a piece between the king and the checking piece.

DIAGRAM 1

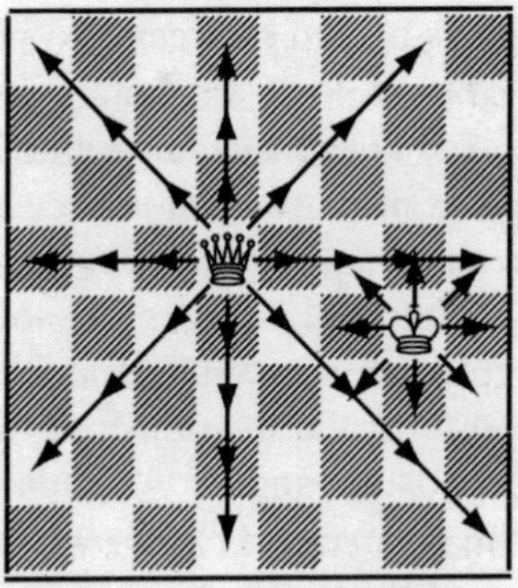

THE KING AND QUEEN

Not all these resources may be available. If none is playable – that is, if the king has no square to which to move out of check, the attacking piece may not be captured and no piece can block the check – then the king is said to be "checkmated", or, simply "mated", and the game is over. Note that the king is the only piece that can never *actually* be captured – the game is concluded when capture is inevitable.

A king may capture an opposing piece by moving onto the square on which it stands, simultaneously removing it from the board. Since it is illegal for the king to move into check, only an undefended piece may be so captured. Capturing in chess is not compulsory (as in draughts), and there is no "huffing" or jumping over the captured piece. The two kings must not stand on adjacent squares, since both would then be in check from each other.

The Queen ♕♛

The queen moves in any direction across any number of vacant squares (diagram 1). Her move is an extension of the king's move, limited only by the confines of the board. She is the most powerful piece on the board.

The queen captures in the same manner as the king but, since she is not liable to check, she may capture a piece that is defended, although such movement is unusual, as, being the most powerful piece, the queen is rarely surrendered voluntarily for a piece other than the opposing queen. It will be seen that the queen, if centrally placed, controls twenty-seven squares on an empty board.

The Rook ♖♜

The rook, sometimes referred to as the castle, may move in a *vertical* or *horizontal* direction only, over any number of vacant squares (diagram 2). It captures in the same manner as the queen, occupying the square on which the hostile piece stands, whilst removing it from the board. Note that wherever a rook stands on an empty board, it commands fourteen squares.

The Bishop ♗♝

The bishop moves *diagonally* only, over any number of vacant squares, capturing in the same manner as the preceding pieces (diagram 2). Note that a bishop is restricted to squares of one colour, and that the nearer it stands to the edge of the board, the fewer the squares it controls.

DIAGRAM 2

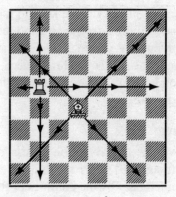

THE ROOK AND THE BISHOP

From the foregoing it will be clear that the queen combines the moves of rook and bishop. If the queen is moved vertically or horizontally over an odd number of squares, she will then command diagonals of the opposite colour, a property with which the bishop is not endowed.

The Knight ♘♞

The move of the knight causes some beginners difficulty. The move is best defined as from one corner of a 3 x 2 rectangle to the opposite corner. Diagram 3 should make this clear.

Pieces standing on intervening squares do not affect the knight's move. For this reason, some players talk of a knight jumping over other pieces.

The knight captures in occupying, as is the case with the other pieces. It is strongest on a crowded board, when it can pursue its designs unimpeded, and is very much weaker on an open board when the mobility of the other pieces is proportionately increased.

It will be noted, also, that the knight, like the king, queen

DIAGRAM 3

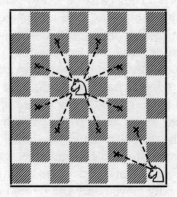

THE KNIGHT

and bishop, controls fewer squares when stationed on or near the edge of the board. Also, that if on a white square it controls only black squares and vice versa.

Until the knight becomes familiar, it is not easy to anticipate its movements and in consequence there is a tendency amongst beginners to over-estimate its powers.

The Pawn ♙ ♟

The pawn, unlike the others, moves in a forward direction only, one square a time.

Each pawn has, however, the option of moving two squares forward on its first move, and this right is retained throughout the game.

The pawn, alone of all the pieces, captures in a different way from which it moves. Whereas it *moves* one square straight forward, it *captures* one square diagonally forward. A pawn may not move diagonally forward unless, in so doing, it captures an opposing piece; nor may it move straight forward, either one or two squares, unless such squares are vacant.

The initial double move of the pawn was introduced to stimulate what would otherwise be a slow game. However, in order that a pawn should not take advantage of the double move to evade a hostile pawn, a rule, known as the *en passant* (French: "in passing") rule was introduced.

This lays down that if a pawn, moving two squares forward from its initial position, could have been captured by an opposing pawn *if it had only moved one square*, then such capture may be made as if the pawn had only moved one square. The pawn making the initial double move is removed from the board and the capturing pawn occupies the square that the captured pawn would have occupied had it only moved one. The right to make a capture *en passant* is forfeited if not exercised immediately. Note that a pawn can only be captured *en passant* by another pawn.

A pawn on reaching the end of the board (the last rank of eight squares) is promoted to any piece (other than a king) that the player chooses. A queen is the natural selection, in view of her being the strongest piece, but occasionally the peculiarity of the position demands promotion to knight, or even to bishop or rook.

No restriction is placed on the number of pawn promotions but, although eight such promotions are possible, it is very rare that more than one or two occur in a game.

Examine diagram 4. In this, as in all other diagrams in the book (and commonly in all chess literature) White is assumed to be playing UP the board, Black DOWN the board. For purposes of economy, four positions are given in one diagram, but in each case the whole of the board is assumed to be included.

In (a) none of the four pawns can move. In (b) the white pawn can capture either the rook or the bishop, or it can move straight ahead onto the white square. In each of these cases it has reached the eighth rank, or end of the board, and must be simultaneously promoted to a piece which is placed on the

DIAGRAM 4

BLACK

(a)   (b)

(c)   (d)

WHITE

THE PAWN

square to which the pawn moves. If a queen is desired, and the white queen is still on the board, an inverted rook or a coin will serve the purpose.

In (c) the white pawns stand in their initial positions, as will be clear from diagram 5. Hence the two outside pawns can both be advanced one or two squares. Both can also capture the black pawn. The black pawn can capture either of these two pawns, whilst the middle white pawn is unable to move.

In (d) the white pawn has just made the initial double move, and Black can consequently capture *en passant* as shown.

In contrast to knights, pawns tend to be underestimated by beginners. Do not shed pawns lightly: every one is a potential queen. Between strong players, an extra pawn on one side is often enough to force victory.

Initial Position

Having seen how the pieces move, let us now set them up in their initial positions, before the start of a game (diagram 5).

Note that the board is positioned so that there is a black square in the left-hand corner of each player.

In the four corners of the board are the rooks, next to them the knights, then the bishops and finally the royal couples – the queens on the squares of their own colour (black queen on black square, white queen on white square).

Notice carefully the asymmetrical arrangement of the kings and queens – each piece opposite its rival counterpart. The pawns are placed in front of the other pieces.

In chess, White always moves first (choice of colour is decided by lot: it is common for one player to conceal two pawns, one white and one black in clenched fists, the

DIAGRAM 5

BLACK

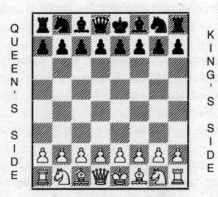

WHITE

THE INITIAL POSITION

opponent then choosing "which hand" to determine colours). Before we can start playing an actual game, however, there are one or two more important rules to be learned; after which it will be necessary to become familiar with a few basic ideas. Chess, to be learnt properly, must be studied step by step, each point being thoroughly assimilated before passing on to the next one, too rapid advancement leading only to confusion and eventual frustration.

Castling

Castling is a privilege to which both sides are entitled once in a game. The manoeuvre, which is a joint move of king and one rook, counts as a single move. It may be played only if all the following conditions are fulfilled:

1. Neither the king nor the rook has moved.
2. The king is not in check.
3. There are no pieces, either hostile or friendly, between the king and the rook, nor does an enemy piece attack a square over which, or onto which, the king must move.

There is a misconception that you may not castle once the king has been in check. This is incorrect: provided that, in getting out of check the king was not moved (thereby contravening (1) above), castling is permitted.

In castling, the king is first moved two squares in the direction of the rook, which then jumps over the king to the next square. The move is then complete.

Castling may take place on either side of the board, and is referred to as king-side castling and queen-side castling. Once castling is complete, the pieces reassume their normal functions and the manoeuvre cannot be retracted.

The object of the move is two-fold: to bring a rook into play in the centre of the board and to give greater security to the king. The manoeuvre is commonly used by both players during a game.

DIAGRAM 6

BLACK

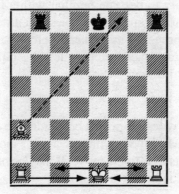

WHITE

CASTLING

Examine diagram 6. White may castle on *either* side (the movements of the pieces are indicated by arrows), whereas Black may not castle at all, since the rook on the queen-side has been moved, and to castle king-side the black king would have to pass over a square controlled by an enemy piece (the white bishop).

Checkmate

We have seen that if a king is attacked (in check) and cannot be moved out of check, and the attacking piece cannot be captured or a friendly piece interposed, the king is assumed to be captured (checkmated, or mated) and the game is over.

Here are four examples in each of which the black king is mated. In diagram 7(a) the black king is attacked by the white queen, which also controls all the neighbouring squares. Since the white queen is protected by the white king, she may not be

DIAGRAM 7

BLACK

(a)   (b)

(c)   (d)

WHITE

CHECKMATE

captured, and Black has consequently lost the game. In (b) the black king is attacked by the advanced white pawn, which is defended by the second white pawn. The knight controls the two remaining squares adjacent to the king ("the king's field"), who is therefore checkmated.

In (c) the black king is again attacked, this time by the white bishop, which also indirectly guards the rook, as if the black king captured the rook he would still be in check, and, as we have seen, this would constitute an illegal move. The white rook controls no fewer than four of the squares in the king's field, the only two remaining escape squares being occupied by black pieces. The pawn is unable to move (remember, White is playing UP the board, Black is playing DOWN), and the black bishop, only capable of moving on white squares, is unable to intervene. Both the black pieces are restricting the movements of the black king.

In (d) the position is more complex and should be examined carefully. The black king is attacked by the white rook, which is also indirectly defending the knight. The white king controls two escape squares, the bishop one and the knight one. Neither the black rook nor the black knight can capture the attacking piece, nor can either interpose between it and the black king. Black is checkmated. Note that if the black rook and knight were interchanged, either of them would be able to move onto the black square between the black king and the hostile rook. If, in the position given, the black knight was not on the board, the black king would still be checkmated, since the white knight attacks the vacated square.

If the black rook was off the board, however, the black king would be able to move out of check into the corner. All the white pieces are indispensable to the mate.

Stalemate

Occasionally a position arises (usually when there are only a few pieces left on the board) when one side, whose turn it is to move, is unable to do so. If the king were in check, the position would be checkmate. If, however, the king is not in check, the game is declared a draw by stalemate.

In diagram 8(a) the white queen controls the three squares in the king's field, *but she is not attacking the king*. If Black has no other pieces on the board, the position would be stalemate with Black to move. In (b), similarly, the bishops control the king's escape squares. Neither the pawn nor the king can move, and if it is Black's turn to play, White is said to have stalemated Black and the game is a draw.

In (c), the black king's only square is next to the white king – to occupy which would be an illegal move. A move by the black bishop would expose the king to an attack from the white rook – again illegal. The black rook is in the same dilemma, any move exposing the king to check from the white bishop. These two black pieces are said to be "pinned". As neither can move, with Black's turn to play, the game is

DIAGRAM 8

BLACK

(a)   (b)

(c)   (d)

WHITE

STALEMATE

drawn. If it were White's turn to play, however, the bishop could capture the rook delivering checkmate.

In (d) it will be seen that none of the black pieces can move – the pawns obstructing the pieces. Black, to play, is stalemated. The possibility of such a position as this occurring in an actual game is remote.

Stalemates are not common in chess, although the threat of stalemate (or, rather, self-stalemate) by the player with the weaker force is often encountered.

Other Methods of Concluding a Game

Apart from checkmate and stalemate, there are several other ways by which a game may be concluded.

1. Insufficient Force

If neither side has sufficient force left to checkmate the opposing king, the game is drawn. What constitutes insufficient force will be explained in the next chapter.

2. Repetition of Moves

If the same position occurs three times in a game, with the same player to move in each case, either side may claim a draw. If this happens as the result of one side submitting the enemy king to a perpetual series of checks, it is usually referred to as "perpetual check". Clearly it will not be to the advantage of the stronger side to resort to a "perpetual" (as perpetual check is more commonly called).

3. Fifty Move Rule

If each side has played 50 consecutive moves without making a capture or pawn move, either player may, on turn, claim a draw. This rule is designed to limit aimless play.

4. Draw by Mutual Agreement

A draw may be agreed between the players at any stage of the game. Positions are often reached where neither player can lay claim to a winning advantage, and both players are reluctant to embark on doubtful ventures. In such positions, a draw is commonly agreed. A high percentage of master games finish in this way.

5. Resignation

A player who sees the position is hopeless, and that checkmate is inevitable sooner or later, will "resign" (concede) the game. More than half of all chess games conclude in this manner.

In point of fact, it is advisable for the beginner not to resign, as more can be learnt from being checkmated a few dozen times. Later, however, resignation in hopeless positions is desirable. A few novices consider that holding out to the bitter end constitutes courage. On the contrary, chess etiquette requires that a player who is clearly beaten should resign in good grace. A player who continues the struggle can only be prolonging the game in the hope that his opponent will make a mistake – a discourteous imputation of an adversary's ability. But, to repeat, every game should be played to a finish in the initial stages of instruction.

In addition to those given above, there are some other ways in which the result of a game may be determined. These, however, have only to do with such matters as the players' conduct and necessary legal niceties associated with match and tournament games, and they need not concern us here.

Chess Notation

It is one of the merits of chess that moves can be recorded. We are thereby not only the fortunate inheritors of the great games of past generations but we also have access to the day-by-day battles of modern masters. In the comfort of your own home you can recreate world championship encounters and, if you wish, keep a record of your own games for future amusement or study.

Systems of recording moves are known as notations. There are two common notations: the Standard (Algebraic), now in general use and alone sanctioned by the International Chess Federation, and the Descriptive (or English) notation, commonly seen in older chess books. The Descriptive notation and the Forsyth notation (used for recording positions) are explained in Chapter 9.

The Standard Notation

It is convenient, for reference purposes, to divide the chessboard into eight files (vertical lines of eight squares) and eight ranks (horizontal lines of eight squares). In the algebraic notation the files are lettered a to h from left to right and the ranks are numbered from 1 to 8 bottom to top, starting from the near left-hand corner of the board when seen from White's side (see diagram 9). Thus every square of the chessboard can be described by a unique letter-and-number (in that order) combination. For example, in the starting position (diagram 5) White's queen stands on d1 and Black's king on e8. The board is also notionally divided vertically into two halves, the king's side and the queen's side. Viewed from White's side, the king's side is the right half of the board and the queen's side the left half. We have already met this distinction in our discussion of castling.

The pieces are identified in algebraic notation by their initial letters: K (king); Q (queen); R (rook); B (bishop); and N (knight to distinguish it from the king); the pawn is not identified (which is itself an identification).

Chess Moves

We now have a system for identifying pieces and squares. All that is needed in addition in order to record games is a few symbols to indicate different types of moves. Just to confuse things a little, there are two types of notation, the long and the short. The only difference between them is that in the long version a move is described in full, whereas in the short version the move is abbreviated. The long is now little used as it is cumbersome and takes up more space. However, since it is clearer it will be used until Chapter 3 when a switch will be made to the shortened form.

In the long version, the initial of the piece is given first followed by the square on which it stands. Then a dash (–) to indicate a move to a vacant square, followed by the description of the square moved to. If a piece is captured in the process, the dash is replaced by a cross (x) to indicate this. Notice that no ambiguity can arise because no more than one piece can ever occupy a square.

Other symbols, common to both long and short notations, are:

+ or ch	= check
# or mate	= checkmate
0-0	= castles (king's side)
0-0-0	= castles (queen's side)

and by way of annotation:

! (exclamation mark)	= good move
!!	= excellent move
? (question mark)	= bad move
??	= very bad move, blunder
!?	= interesting move
?!	= dubious or risky move

The *en passant* capture is abbreviated: e.p.

Now for a few examples. Look at diagram 9. If in this position White advanced the pawn at a2 two squares, the move would be transcribed a2–a4; while if instead this pawn

DIAGRAM 9

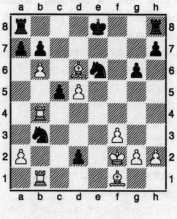

STANDARD NOTATION

captured the knight, the move would be recorded as a2xb3. If White checks with the bishop (only one bishop can check), the move would be Bf1–b5+. If Black chose to move the queen's rook next to the king, the description would be Ra8–d8 while, if the advanced black pawn is promoted to queen, this move would be recorded as d2–d1Q. At first, this may seem a bit complicated but fluency will come with a little practice.

Conclusion

If you have read this chapter at a single sitting, you will probably be in a state of near mental exhaustion. You have possibly already forgotten how the knight moves, or what stalemate is; but you should not let this worry you.

You have the consolation of knowing that there are only a few very minor rules still to be learned, the rest of the book being devoted to the right way to play the game.

The chapter should be re-read carefully after a short interval, and before going on you should be thoroughly conversant with the moves of the pieces, pawn promotion, check and checkmate, stalemate, castling and chess notation. A good idea is to place half a dozen pieces haphazardly on the board and move them around, black and white alternately, capturing, checking, and, if possible, securing positions in which checkmate or stalemate may be given. Then try recording moves as you go along.

By way of a test, return to diagram 9 and see how many of the following questions you can answer correctly (the answers appear on page 32).

1. How many pieces in the position given are unable to move?
2. To how many squares can the white bishop on d6 move?
3. How many white pieces are on their original squares?
4. Can White play Kf2–e1?
5. If Black captures the pawn on b6 with the pawn at a7, how should this move be recorded?
6. On the whole board, how many possible (i.e. legal) black moves are there? (Count the pawn promotion as one move.)

Solutions to Test (Chapter 1)

1. One. The black pawn at b7.
2. Eight, including the pawn capture.
3. Ten: White Bf1, Pa2, Pg2, Ph2.
    Black Ke8, Ra8, Rh8, Pa7, Pb7, Ph7
4. No: because the white king would then be in check from the black pawn.
5. a7xb6
6. Twenty-nine.

2

BASIC THEORY

Relative Values of the Chess Pieces

The reader will no doubt have gathered by this time that the chess pieces, being possessed of intrinsic qualities of movement and capture, may also be compared, one with the other, on the yardstick of relative values.

The correlation of the powers of the pieces is deceptive, however, as in any position each piece will be possessed of a power peculiar to that position. In diagram 9, page 29, for example, both black rooks are out of play, whereas the humble pawn on d2, threatening, if unwatched, to become a queen, is an apparent force. However, the pawn may soon fall, and the black rooks may bring their long-range guns to bear down the vital files. A game is therefore in a permanent state of flux, and the values of the pieces change from move to move. The scale of relative values can only remain a guide for the exchange of pieces (an exchange is when one side captures an opposing piece, giving up one of its own pieces in the process) when other considerations are approximately equal. The ability to assess the true value of a position and, in consequence, the temporary values of the pieces composing the position, is a gift with which only really strong chess players are endowed.

The king, since he cannot be captured, and is only used as

an attacking piece towards the end of the game when his powers are approximately equal to those of a bishop, is excluded from the assessment.

Queen = 9 points
Bishop or knight = 3 points or 3 pawns
Rook = 5 points (or a bishop/knight and 2 pawns)

These are approximations. The bishop is normally worth a fraction more than the knight (although there are many positions where knights are stronger than bishops). The queen is perhaps slightly undervalued in this table, but two rooks working together are usually slightly stronger than the queen.

Basic Positions
(a) The Pin
As we have seen in position (c), diagram 8, page 25, a piece is pinned if, in moving, it would expose the king to a hostile check. In diagram 10(a), the knight is also said to be pinned, for although it may be legally moved, the white bishop would then capture the black queen which would be a poor bargain for Black even should the bishop be captured.

The term "pin" is thus extended to signify any position in which the movement of a piece would expose an undefended piece to attack, or a stronger piece to attack from a weaker piece. If there was another black knight at c7 (that is, on the diagonal between the queen and the other knight), the set-up would be known as a half-pin as the movement of either knight would automatically result in the pinning of the other.

(b) Double Check
In the second example (diagram 10(b)), we see a double check, when a king is exposed to attack from two hostile pieces simultaneously. White has just moved the rook, as indicated. In a double check the king must move, since he cannot capture both attacking pieces or interpose two of his own pieces in one move.

DIAGRAM 10

BLACK

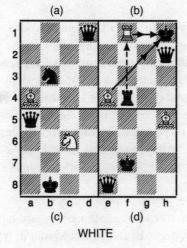

(a)   (b)

(c)   (d)

WHITE

BASIC TACTICS

If he cannot move, as in diagram 10(b), he is checkmated. Note that Black can apparently capture either piece with the rook, or interpose a piece between either the king and rook or the king and bishop, but none of these resources is open to him because, whichever he adopts, the king will still be in check from the remaining white piece.

The extraordinary power of the double check is apparent, and it is something a player should endeavour to avoid unless he is certain that such check would be innocuous – which is very rarely the case.

(c) Discovered Check
This is similar to the double check, but not as dangerous, as the piece moved does not itself give check. If in diagram 10(b), the white rook had moved to f7 instead of f8 it would then have been

a "discovered" and not a "double" check. Black could thus have avoided mate, but would have lost the queen.

(d) The Fork

The knight, by virtue of its irregular move, can create an embarrassing attack known as a "fork". In the position 10(c), the knight is attacking both king and queen, and as the king must move out of check, the queen is doomed. The most common fork of the knight is of king and rook, when the rook, which, as we have seen, is the stronger piece, is lost. Forks by other pieces are possible. In diagram 4(b), on page 19, for example, the white pawn has forked the black rook and bishop. The term is self-explanatory.

(e) The Skewer

The position in 10(d) is something to guard against. Here the black king, in check, is compelled to move, when the bishop will capture the black queen.

Endings

In order to acquaint the reader with the practical power of the pieces, we will examine one or two game endings.

Assuming that Black has only a king left, White will be able to force mate with a minimum force of:

1. King and queen. The white king will, of course, be on the board. If White has a pawn which he can safely promote, then it can be reckoned as a queen.
2. King and rook.
3. King and two bishops.
4. King, bishop and knight.

Mate cannot be forced against a lone king with:

1. King alone – this is obvious.
2. King and bishop.

3. King and knight or king and two knights.

It is interesting to observe that two knights (the joy of the novice!) are unable to force mate, whereas a mere pawn which can be promoted is sufficient for the purpose.

King and Queen v King
Let us examine the system of forcing mate by king and queen against a bare king.

This performance should not demand more than ten moves, in most positions considerably fewer (when we talk about moves in chess we mean moves of both sides).

Place the white king on e1, the white queen on e8, and the black king on g5. White can mate in a number of ways, but the principle remains the same in every case – the lone king must be driven to the edge of the board where the queen will deliver the mate, the white king assisting.

A series of checks with the queen will achieve nothing. (All beginners assume that checks are stronger than quiet moves (i.e. moves that are not checks), in the hope, presumably, that "it might be mate".) White, therefore, moves Qe8–f7!, restricting the movements of the doomed monarch.

Notice that in chess, moves are numbered in pairs.

	White	*Black*
1.	Qe8–f7	Kg5–g4

Not Kg5–h4, when Qf7–g6 further restricts the king.

2.	Ke1–f2	Kg4–g5
3.	Kf2–g3	Kg5–hg

The only square.

| 4. | Qf7–g8 | |

4. Kg3–f4? would be a grave error since the black king would then be without a move – stalemated, in other words – and the game would be drawn.

    4. **...**   **Kh6–h5**

Again the only move.

    5. Kg3–f4   **Kh5–h6**

Not Kh5–h4 allowing White to mate immediately.

    6. Kf4–f5

And now mate next move is unavoidable.

    6. **...**   **Kh6–h5**
    7. Qg8–g5#

The black king has been forced to the edge of the board and is there checkmated. King and queen cannot mate a bare king anywhere except at the side: the same applies to king and rook against bare king, as the following example shows.

King and Rook v King
Set up the kings as before, and substitute a white rook for the queen. Since this mate is more difficult, as might be expected, and as it is one which you are likely to encounter (if your opponent obstinately refuses to resign), it is essential to be familiar with the correct procedure.

        White   *Black*
    1. Re8–f8

Limiting the black king.

1.	...	Kg5–g4
2.	Ke1–e2	Kg4–g3
3.	Ke2–e3	Kg3–g4
4.	Rf8–f1	Kg4–g5

Black is playing the best defence.

5.	Ke3–e4	Kg5–g6
6.	Ke4–e5	Kg6–g7
7.	Ke5–e6	Kg7–g6
8.	Rf1–g1+	

The king is now forced to the edge of the board. Note the position of the white king at the precise moment of the check: it is directly opposite the black king, thereby controlling the three squares between them that would otherwise have been open to the fugitive. The black king is now confined to the h file. White aims to set up the same position to deliver checkmate.

8.	...	Kg6–h5
9.	Ke6–f5	Kh5–h4
10.	Rg1–g8	Kh4–h3
11.	Kf5–f4	Kh3–h2
12.	Kf4–f3	Kh2–h1
13.	Kf3–f2	Kh1–h2

The black king is forced to face the white king: the curtain falls.

14. Rg8–h8#

The maximum number of moves required for this type of ending is seventeen – and this only in extreme cases.

King and two Rooks v King

This is a very easy ending, the two rooks being moved rank by rank or file by file, to the edge of the board where the lone king is checkmated.

Place the white king on e1, the two white rooks on a1 and h1, and the black king on e4. White mates in eight moves by:
1. Ra1–a3 Ke4–f4 2. Rh1–h4+ Kf4–g5 3. Rh4–b4 Kg5–f5
4. Ra3–a5+ Kf5–e6 5. Rb4–b6+ Ke6–d7 6. Ra5–a7+ Kd7–c8
7. Ra7–h7 Kc8–d8 8. Rb6–b8#.

This is not the quickest way to force mate but it is the easiest to understand.

King and two Bishops v King

The ending with king and two bishops embraces the same idea of driving the lone king to the edge of the board, the pieces working in conjunction to cut off the escape squares (or flight squares, as they are more commonly called). The king must be mated on a corner square, and in this respect the mate differs from the endings with queen and rook given above.

King, Bishop and Knight v King

The ending with king, bishop and knight against bare king is conducted in the same manner as the ending with the two bishops, except that the victim must be mated on a corner square of the same colour as that on which the bishop stands.

Most elementary textbooks on chess give pages of analysis on these two endings which serve only to bewilder the student. Many experienced players are unable to force the mate with bishop and knight. And, indeed, why worry? This ending is very rare in actual play and the procedure is beyond the scope of this book.

King and Pawn Endings

When the tumult of the middle game has subsided into the comparative quiet of the end game, it is usual for each side to be left with three or four pieces. With only a few pieces remaining it is easier to calculate with precision the best line of play – indeed, the end game of chess is a fine art, and there are many books devoted to this subject alone.

With only a limited force available, it is unlikely that either king is in danger of being mated. The play is therefore concentrated on the task of queening (promoting) pawns – which does not mean to say that either player should lose sight of mating possibilities.

As soon as one side succeeds in promoting a pawn, he will obviously have a decided, if not decisive, advantage, and can then turn his attention to destroying the enemy force preparatory to the final checkmate.

On a crowded board the likelihood of a pawn surviving the hazardous march from the second to the eighth rank is remote; but, as the forces decrease, its power augments. It will be seen, therefore, that in the end game the pawn takes on a new importance, since the longer it survives, the greater are its chances of eventual promotion.

To understand even the simplest end games, it is necessary to study the movements of the pawn in conjunction with the movements of the two kings.

Look at diagram 11. Here are four simple examples of king and pawn endings.

In (a) Black to move is a draw, since the king is stalemated. White, to move, wins, however. 1. Kb6–c6 Kb8–a7 (the only move) 2. Kc6–c7 (still guarding the pawn and preventing Black returning to the promotion square) Ka7–a6 3. b7–b8Q and White mates in two more moves.

In (b) Black to move is a draw (stalemate). If White to move, he is in a quandary. The only square to which he can play the king and still guard the pawn (g6) leaves the black king in stalemate, whilst any other king move permits Black to capture the pawn. From which we derive the important precept that if, in a king and rook's pawn v king ending, the solitary king can reach the queening square before the pawn, the game is drawn.

DIAGRAM 11

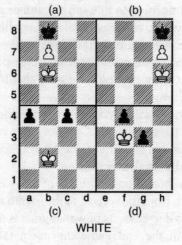

PAWN-PLAY

The difference between 11(a) and 11(b) will now be apparent. In (a) the white king penetrates by forcing the black king out on the opposite file; whereas in (b) he is not able to do this.

In (c) the king is unable to capture either pawn without permitting the other to queen. For example, 1. Kb2–c3 a4–a3 2. Kc3xc4 a3–a2 and queens (promotes to queen) next move. The white king can only shuffle impotently between b2 and b1 until the black king arrives on the scene to force the issue. Black loses both pawns in an attempt to promote one without assistance:

1. Kb2–b1 c4–c3 2. Kb1–c2 a4–a3 3. Kc2xc3 a3–a2 4. Kc3–b2.

In (d) White can again do nothing but move his king around until the black king arrives. If he captures the unprotected pawn, he cannot stop the other one queening.

Promotion Square

A simple rule for determining whether a pawn, advancing alone to promotion, can be captured by the king before it reaches the queening square, is illustrated in diagram 12.

Imagine a square with one side marking out the path from pawn to queening square. If the black king can move inside this square, he can capture the pawn. In the diagram, Black, with the move, draws by playing Kb3–c3 or c4. White, with the move, wins by h3–h4, and the pawn cannot be stopped. If the pawn were at h2, White would still win by virtue of the initial double pawn move 1. h2–h4. This rule only applies to a pawn advancing alone: if the White king or other piece can in any way influence the play, the formula does not apply.

DIAGRAM 12

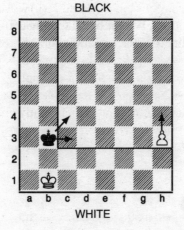

THE QUEENING SQUARE

Conclusion

You should now have a reasonable grasp of the elementary principles of the game. In order that you may not become over-wearied with theory, we shall proceed to play over a short game or two, assessing the value of each move as we go.

Before passing on, however, try the following brief test based on the points we have examined (answers on page 46):

1. Place WK on a8, WN on e3; BK on h6, BQ on h2, BB on b8. Black plays Bb8–a7 attacking the knight and threatening Qh2–b8#. What result?
2. In the king and queen ending given in this chapter, after Black played 6. . . . Kh6–h5, White mated by 7. Qg8–g5. Can you see any alternative mates for White in this position (one move)?
3. Place WK on a1, WP on a4; BK on f5. Can Black, to move, prevent the WP queening?
4. Place WK on d6, WR on d1; BK on e8. White to play. Mate in how many moves?
5. Place WK on h5, WP on f7; BK on h7. White to play. What result?
6. Place WK on b5, WP on b6; BK on b8. (i) White to move – what result? (ii) Black to move – what result?

Solutions to Test (Chapter 2)

1. Draw. White can play Ne3–g4+! forking king and queen, thus leaving both sides with insufficient mating force. If White plays Ka8xa7?, Black plays simply Qh2–f2 pinning the knight, capturing it next move and winning easily with king and queen against king.

2. Qg8–h8 or h7 – here the queen, notice, is only exercising her powers as a rook.

3. Yes, by Kf5–e6, e5 or e4.

4. Two: 1. Rd1–f1! Ke8–d8 2. Rf1–f8#.

5. White wins: 1. f7–f8R etc. Not 1. f7–f8Q stalemate, or 1. f7–f8B or N with insufficient mating force. Black to play draws by Kh7–g7 winning the pawn.

6. Draw in each case. (i) 1. Kb5–a6 Kb8–a8 (not 1. . . . Kb8–c8? 2. Ka6–a7); 2. b6–b7+ Ka8–b8 and White must now give up the pawn or stalemate the black king. (ii) 1 . . . Kb8–b7! and White can do nothing except move about on the fifth rank as Black alternates between b8 and b7. If the white king tries to penetrate, the sequel is as in (i). Note that 1. . . . Kb8–a8 (or c8) would be fatal: 2. Kb5–a6 (or c6) Ka8–b8 3. b6–b7 wins (see diagram 11(a)). On examination it will be seen that if one side can play a pawn to the seventh rank in this type of ending *without giving check*, and provided that the pawn is not a rook's pawn, he will win.

3

EXAMPLES OF PLAY

The object of the game, we know, is to checkmate the opposing king. Since a direct assault is not always possible (and might result in placing your own king in jeopardy) other, more immediate targets, must be found.

Four factors dominate the play:

1. Time – represented by the moves of the pieces.
2. Force – represented by the powers of the pieces.
3. Space – represented by the territory controlled by the pieces.
4. Position – represented by such factors as king safety and pawn structure.

A gain in time (or "tempo" as it is called), by forcing your opponent to waste moves, will often permit you to marshal your forces effectively and swiftly.

A gain in force by, say, trading an enemy rook for a bishop or a knight (known as "winning the exchange") is clearly advantageous. Other things being equal, a material advantage of one pawn or its equivalent will often be enough for victory, and a larger material advantage will almost always be enough.

A gain in space – extending your territorial control, thereby achieving greater manoeuvrability for your pieces – is again usually an advantage.

When other factors are equal, a positional advantage such as a safer king or a superior pawn structure can often be decisive.

Bearing these four points in mind, in addition to the ultimate aim of mating the opposing king, every move in a game should be made to some purpose.

If you have no plan, and aimlessly shift pieces around as the fancy takes you, you will rarely hold out for longer than a dozen or so moves. Better – far better – to have a bad plan than to have no plan at all. That does not mean that a course of action, once formulated, should be adhered to obstinately; but rather that it should be modified or recast if necessary to meet changing conditions.

Remember, therefore, to play with a purpose at all times.

In chess, as in war, movements are governed by two determining factors – strategy and tactics. Strategy can be said to consist of the spadework; tactics, which implements strategy, the point-to-point struggle.

Some players prefer the subtleties of finer strategy, others the exhilarating rough-and-tumble of tactical play; it is this distinction which to a greater or lesser degree determines a player's style.

So much for theory, and we are now ready to play over an actual game. The pieces are set up as in diagram 5, page 20 (black square left-hand corner!) and White moves first.

From hereon the short algebraic will be used. In this notation, the square from which a piece moves is omitted, as is the dash. Thus Bf1–e2 is recorded simply as Be2. Sometimes ambiguity can arise. Look back at diagram 9, page 29. Assume White captures the black knight at b3 with the rook at b4. Rxb4 is not good enough because it is not clear which rook is taking the knight. In situations like this, either the rank (in this case) or the file on which the piece to be moved stands is given immediately after the initial letter. So the move would be written R4xb3. Similarly, if Black moves the knight e6 to d4, the move would be Ned4 since the knight at b3 could also move there. As the pawn is not identified by a letter, a move such as g2–g4 becomes simply g4. When a pawn makes a capture, the file on which the pawn stands is given first; thus d5xe6 is rendered dxe6, or sometimes simply dxe.

	White	*Black*
1.	**e4**	

An excellent move. Note that the king's bishop and the queen are now free (in the initial position only the pawns and the knights are able to move). This pawn advance also strikes at the centre, which is the most important area of the board and the focus of all opening play.

1. ...   **e5**

The same. One of Black's best replies. Clearly it achieves the same as White's move. Note that now neither of these pawns can move.

2. Nf3

The king's knight is brought into play. It attacks the black pawn and is therefore an aggressive move. It also attacks the d4 square.

2. ...   **Nc6**

Obvious and best. The pawn is now guarded, and the knight counter attacks the d4 square. It will be observed that the game to this point has revolved round the four centre squares. The struggle for these squares, control of which always yields the superior game, motivates most opening manoeuvres.

3. a4

A very weak move indeed: it demonstrates White has no

plan. It does not serve a single useful function, being far removed from the central squares. White has dissipated the advantage of the extra move.

3. ...   **Nf6**

A good move, it continues the assault on the centre, attacking White's e-pawn.

4. Qe2

Bad. Although this move protects the threatened pawn, it hinders the development of the king's bishop. Bd3 in this position would have been no better, since then the queen's pawn would have been unable to move and White would have experienced difficulty in getting the queen's bishop out. Nc3 was correct.

4. ...   **Bc5**

Another good move which develops a piece and attacks the d4 square.

5. g3

White sees that he is unable to develop the bishop on the long diagonal, and seeks to bring it into play via g2.

5. ...   **d6**

Black's queen's bishop is now able to come into the game.

6. Bg2

The bishop is now said to be "fianchettoed" in the jargon of the chess player. In some parts of the world, where the double pawn move wasn't accepted, it was usual to develop the bishops in this manner, since the centre pawns, only capable of moving one square at a time, would free one bishop only to block the other.

White could not, of course, play 6. Bh3 here, as the piece would then have been undefended, permitting Black to play Bxh3, winning a clear piece for nothing.

6. ...	0-0

Castles. The black king is now in comparative safety, and the rook is brought into the game.

Up to here Black's moves have been an example of model play. At some points he has had the choice of several good moves, whilst other moves could have been transposed, but his play could hardly have been improved upon.

The position in diagram 13 (overleaf) has now been reached. Check this with your board to ensure that the two agree. A quick assessment of the game as it stands reveals that White has decidedly the worst of it. The bishop on g2 is doing nothing, the queen is no better placed at e2 than at d1; and the a-pawn, a waif in the wilderness, has achieved nothing by its inconsequential advance.

Black, on the other hand, has his pieces posted to some purpose. His development (i.e. the bringing of his pieces into play) is almost complete, when he will be ready to embark on an attack. The contest may now be said to be entering the middle game. There are three recognized phases in a game of chess: the opening, middle and end game. There is no strict dividing line between them, the opening being understood to consist of the developing moves of each side, the middle game the main struggle, the end game when the majority of the pieces are off the board and the kings and pawns come into their own. We shall study each of these phases separately in ensuing chapters.

7. Qb5

DIAGRAM 13

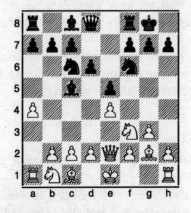

POSITION AFTER BLACK'S 6TH MOVE

Another bad move which threatens nothing; the black bishop, knight and knight's pawn are all protected and the e-pawn is now unguarded. White should have again played Nc3.

7. ...   Nb4!

A very strong move, hence the exclamation mark. (Black could equally well have played simply Nxe4 here.) Black now threatens to play Nxc2+, forking the king and the rook, with considerable material gain.

8. Na3

This guards the c-pawn, which would now make the exchange unfavourable to Black. White could also have played Kd1, but then the f-pawn would have been undefended, and, more important still, White would have forfeited the right to castle. Attacking the knight with c3 would also have been no good, since Black could still have continued Nc2+, winning the exchange at least. Qc4 would have allowed Black to continue Be6! attacking the queen and thereby gaining a "tempo".

8. ...   Bd7

The white queen is attacked. Again, Black could also have captured on e4.

9. Qc4

Note carefully that if, in this position, White had played instead Qxb7, Black would have replied either Rb8! or Bc6! and the queen is without a flight square. White would then have had nothing better than to give up the queen for the rook.

9. ...   Be6

Again attacking the queen and tempting White into making a mistake. Stronger, though, was the immediate Nxe4.

10. Qc3

Observe how an early foray with the queen is quickly punished. It is rarely advisable to bring the major pieces into the middle of the board at the beginning of a game, since they can be constantly harassed by the enemy minor pieces and much time is lost in the process. (The bishops and knights are known as the "minor" pieces, the rooks and queens as "major" pieces.) This move turns out to be very bad, as will be seen. Correct was Qe2.

10. ...   Nxe4

The queen is trapped.

11. d4

White opens the game – too late.

11. ...　　　　　　　　　exd4

There is no hurry to take the queen off – she is still not able to escape. Note that the king's file is now open for Black's rook.

12. Nxd4　　　　　　　　Nxc3
13. bxc3

As the result of this move White has what is known as "doubled pawns" – two pawns on the same file. The a-pawn is now isolated, and is called an "isolated pawn". Both these are weaknesses which we shall examine at a later stage; White's game is lost anyway.

13. ...　　　　　　　　　Re8
14. cxb4

Ignoring the "discovered check" which is threatened by Black moving the bishop on e6, thereby exposing the white king to attack from the rook. Black has time to spare however, and first takes his piece back.

14. ...　　　　　　　　　Bxd4

Attacking the queen's rook. c3 is no defence for White, as Black would play simply Bxc3+, forking king and rook.

15. Rb1

Now Black can play to win material by Ba2+ (a discovered check), when White, who must first deal with the check, will lose his rook. Observe the immense power of a discovered check – the bishop can go anywhere on the board without fear of capture because White must first attend to the attack on his king.

15. . . .   **Bc3+**

Winning easily, but Bh3+ was even stronger. Black does not take full advantage of the position in which there are several good continuations. He is so heavily up in material however – a queen and a pawn for a knight – that it matters little.

16. Kf1

Escaping from the potential discovered check but Bd2 would not have been much better. Kd1 would have been worse: Black can force mate in five moves starting with Bg4+.

16. . . .   **Bc4+!**

Decisive.

17. Kg1

Not Nxc4 Re1#! Black sacrifices the bishop in order to clear the file for the rook. It may be argued that such an offer hardly constitutes a sacrifice. Certainly it is not a sacrifice in the true sense, but chess terminology rules that it shall be so described, so there it is.

The sacrifice is one of the keenest sources of delight to the chess player, the apparent surrender of force creating a whimsical effect which is at once self-satisfying and artistic. This is an example of a tactical sacrifice – by far the most common. The strategic sacrifice – the relinquishing of a piece in order to gain time or space, particularly in the opening – is more common among stronger players as it requires sound judgement.

17. . . .   **Re1+**
18. Bf1

The only move.

18. . . .	Rxf1+
19. Kg2	

The king cannot, of course, take the rook since it is defended by the queen's bishop.

19. . . .	Bd5+
20. Kh3?	

20. Kf1 was the only way to avoid a swift mate, but naturally not 20. f3 Rxf3 when Black would again be threatening a dangerous discovered check.

20. . . .	Qd7+

20. . . . Bf3 was an even quicker way to win.

21. Kh4

21. g4 would have lost immediately to Bf3 when White can only delay Qxg4#.

21. . . .	Bf3

Now mate cannot be avoided. It is often the quiet move rather than the garish check that precedes the climax.

22. Kg5

White could have delayed mate for a few moves by playing 22. h3.

22. . . .	Qg4#

Finis. See diagram 14.

DIAGRAM 14

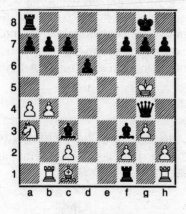

FINAL POSITION

Observations

By normal standards this is a short game, the average being around thirty-five moves. A long game will run to sixty moves and more – occasionally into three figures.

There are a number of lessons to be learned from the play of both sides, but the main cause of White's collapse was his dilatory handling of the opening. It was evident almost from the outset that he had no plan of campaign.

Witness Black's handling of the game by comparison – a polished if not perfect performance.

1. He developed his pieces quickly.
2. He took advantage of White's errors.
3. He wasted no time in side issues.

It is of particular interest to notice that Black succeeded in castling and bringing his king's rook into play, the uncastled white king offering a vulnerable target.

In the final position observe the confusion in the white ranks.

The queen's bishop and king's rook are still "at home"; the queen's knight is posted at the side of the board guarding a threat which for many moves has ceased to exist; the queen's rook has been forced to waste a tempo to avoid the attack of a minor piece; and, of course, that unhappy pawn is still forlornly standing, without rhyme or reason, on a4. A sorry picture!

Three Brevities
The shortest possible game of chess ending in mate is a brevity known as Fool's Mate. It runs to only two moves:

	White	*Black*
1.	**f3**	**e5**
2.	**g4**	**Qh4#**

None of White's king's side pieces is able to interpose.

The term "Fool's Mate" is something of a misnomer, since in his early acquaintance with the game the beginner may easily overlook the vulnerability of his king, particularly when the attacking piece descends "from the blue".

On the other hand, a game concluded in four moves known as the "Scholar's Mate" is much more obvious. White wins this time:

	White	*Black*
1.	**e4**	**e5**
2.	**Bc4**	**Bc5**
3.	**Qh5**	**Nf6**
4.	**Qxf7#**	

If Black had played Nf6 before he brought the bishop out, all would have been well, as Qh5 could then have been met by Nxh5. But in any case Black had nothing to fear if he fathomed White's designs. For example, 3.... Qe7, defending both the threatened mate and the e-pawn was good since, as we have learned from the previous game, White will lose time parrying Black's imminent attacks on the wayward queen.

Variations and extensions of these two mating themes are often encountered. The f-pawn, against which the attack in Scholar's Mate is directed, is the weakest link in the initial position, for it is guarded only by the king. A further point in favour of castling: the rook is brought to the protection of this pawn.

Here is another short game with an attractive sacrifice:

	White	Black
1.	e4	e5
2.	Nf3	d6
3.	Bc4	h6
4.	Nc3	Bg4

Pinning the knight.

5. Nxe5!

The surprise: White sacrifices the queen.

5. ...   Bxd1

This loses, but after 5. . . . dxe4 6. Qxg4 White has won a pawn and is ahead in development.

6. Bxf7+

That weak f-pawn again!

6.	...	Ke7
7.	Nd5#	

Before returning to the study of chess theory, the reader would do well to play over another game and endeavour to answer the questions posed.

Initial position again – black square left-hand corner – queens on the squares of their own colour.

White	Black
1. e4	e5
2. Bc4	

(a) Good or bad?

2. . . .	Na6

(b) Is this better than Nc6?

   3. Nf3

The black pawn is now attacked and is said to be *en prise* (French: "in a position to be taken").

3. . . .	f6?

It is a good general rule that this move is bad in the opening, seriously weakening the king's position.

   4. Nxe5!

A tactical sacrifice.

4. . . .	fxe5

Black would have done much better to decline the sacrifice by playing Qe7.

5. Qh5+	g6

(c) Why not 5. . . . Ke7?

6.	Qxe5+	Qe7
7.	Qxh8	Qxe4+
8.	Be2	

(d) Why not Kd1 or Kf1?

| 8. | ... | Ne7 |

(e) What was White threatening?

| 9. | d3 | Qxg2 |
| 10. | Bh6 | |

Another sacrifice.

| 10. | ... | Qxh1+ |
| 11. | Kd2 | d6 |

(f) Why can't Black play Bxh6+?

| 12. | Qxf8+ | Kd7 |
| 13. | Bg5 | |

A strong move, but even better was 13. Bg4+ Nf5 14. Nc3, when Black has to give up his queen to avoid mate. The black knight is twice attacked, and since it cannot be further protected by another piece, it must move or be captured.

| 13. | ... | Nf5 |

(g) Why not Nc6?

| 14. | Qf7+ | Kc6 |
| 15. | Nc3! | |

Another good sacrifice. The rook is *en prise* to the black queen.

15. ...   Qg2

The only move. Black must keep on the diagonal to prevent the bishop check. If 15. . . . Qxa1? there would follow 16. Bf3+, when Black would be mated in three moves at most. How? (h)

16. Rg1!

A pretty move. The queen's bishop is attacked by the black queen, so White promptly offers the rook again, hoping to decoy the queen off the vital diagonal.

16. ...   Qxf2

Now the white king's bishop is pinned.

17. Rf1

Good enough, but Qe8+ would have been a stronger choice. (i) If 17. Be3, attacking the queen, and guarding the rook, how would Black have continued?

17. ...   Qg2
18. Kd1

(j) Why does White move his king here? In fact Ke1 would have been much better, so that the king could defend the rook.

18. ...   d5

Clearly not 18. . . Ne3+? 19. Bxe3. Or 18. . . . . Kb6 19. Qb3+. Another possible line is 18. . . . Nd4 19. Qc4+ Nc5 (19. . . . Kd7? 20. Rf7+ Ke8 21. Re7+ Kf8 22. Qf7# or

21. . . . Kd8 Qg8#) 20. Bf3+! – yet another sacrifice – Nxf3
21. Qb5#.

19. Nxd5

White should have preferred to save his threatened bishop
with Bf4.

(k) Why not still 19. Bf3?

19. . . .   **Nc5**

Black should have taken the opportunity to take the
proffered bishop on g5, when it is not immediately clear how
White can win the game.

(l) Why not 19. . . Qxd5?

20. Qxc7+

White, offering a further knight, wins at last.

20. . . .   **Kxd5**

(m) Can Black play 20. . . Kb5, declining the tainted gift?

21. Bf3+

White misses a conclusive finish: 21. Rxf5+ B (or g)xf5
22. c4+ Kd4 (22. . . . Ke6 23. Qe7#) 23. Qg7#.

21. . . .   **Qxf3+**
22. Rxf3   **Resigns**

Black has two knights for a queen and a pawn. He has no
chance of redressing the balance, and his king is in the centre
of the board open to continuous attack. Under the circumstances, a graceful surrender is the best course.

Observations

This is the kind of punishment that the student must expect to receive from the strong player. A wasted knight move, an injudicious pawn advance and Black was in trouble.

White sacrificed continually throughout the game and yet won the game. Why? Because on each occasion, he correctly assessed the relative values of the pieces involved, and played accordingly.

Sacrifices of this nature have to be very carefully calculated, however, since a single slip in analysis would prove disastrous.

For this reason, the student is advised not to give up voluntarily even a pawn unless he can foresee the consequences. As you progress, you will often be able to sense a sacrifice, but insight of this nature comes only with practice.

All sacrifices should be treated on their merits alone. Regrettably, this seemingly trite advice is rarely followed. Beginners tend to fall into two classes: those who grab everything on the principle that they then have the superior force and it is incumbent upon the opponent to maintain the initiative; and those who never accept anything on the principle that if a piece is offered it must be a trap.

If you see no objection to accepting a proffered piece, do not hesitate. An apparent sacrifice is often an oversight: the player has simply put or left a piece *en prise*.

Solutions to Test (Chapter 3)

(a)   Good, since it develops a piece, prevents Black playing d5, and attacks the weak f-pawn. The usual rule, and a good one to stick to when learning the game, is "knights and bishops out first".

(b)   No. It is away from the centre of the board. The knight on a6 controls four unimportant squares – exactly half the number of squares it would control on c6.

(c)   Because of Qxe5#!

(d)   Because the bishop is *en prise*.

(e)   9. Qxg8.

(f)   Because the bishop is pinned by the white queen.

(g)   Because of Bg4#

(h)   (1) 16. . . . d5 17. Qxd5+ Kb6 18. Qb5 or Na4#.
        (2) 16. . . . Kc5 17. Qc4 (or d5)+, K moves 18. Qb5#.
        (3) 16. . . . Kb6 17. Qb3+ Nb4 (17. . . . Kc5 18. Qc4+
        Kb6 19. Qb5# or 17. . . . Ka5 18. Qb5#) 18. Qxb4+ Ka6
        19. Qb5#.

(i)   17. . . . Qxe3+ (not 17. . . . Nxe3? 18. Qxf2) 18. Kd1
        Qxg1+ and Black wins easily, being a rook, knight and
        pawn ahead. This move (17. Be3) would have been a
        bad blunder on White's part.

(j)   To unpin the bishop. The move threatens Bf3+, winning
        the queen. White forced Black to capture the f-pawn, a
        sacrifice that permitted the white rook to make use of
        the open file to guard f3 so that the bishop can check.

(k)   Because of 18. . . . Qxf1+.

(l)   Because of 20. Bf3, and the queen is pinned and lost.

(m)   No; Black would then be mated by 21. a4+ Ka6
        22. Nb4. Or 21. . . . Nxa4 22. Qc4+ Ka5 23. b4#; if
        21. . . . Kxa4, White can mate in several ways: 22. Nc3+
        followed by 23. Rf4+ or 22. b3+ followed by 23. Bc1+
        etc. 21. c4+ also mates quickly.

4

POWERS OF THE PIECES

If the previous chapters have been followed carefully, you should now have a good idea of how to play chess. Should you still be uncertain on any point turn back here and dispel any doubts before proceeding further.

The last chapter was devoted to actual games, as a means of breaking the inevitable boredom that the study of page upon page of theory engenders; but now it is necessary to return to the elements of play.

As has been seen, the functions and values of the chess pieces vary from stage to stage individually, collectively and relatively.

It is possible to generalize on the powers and limitations of the various pieces throughout the game, and to lay down broad principles for handling them.

It will be as well to repeat here that the three phases through which a game can pass are:

1. The opening – development of the pieces.
2. The middle game – the main struggle.
3. The end game – the fight for pawn promotion.

A game can be concluded in the opening or the middle game without ever reaching the end game (as in the illustrative examples in Chapter 3), the three divisions having no relation to the duration of a game; that is to say, the end game is not the last moves of any chess game, but specifically that field of play in which the majority of the pieces are off the board and the kings and pawns dominate the play.

Bearing this in mind, let us examine the pieces individually under these three headings.

1.   The Opening
(a) King
The king should be kept closely guarded in the opening, when a surprise attack is always a danger. Early castling is advisable, and in this respect the K-side is to be preferred to the queen's, since after the latter the a-pawn is unprotected.

(b) Queen
It is usually inadvisable to move the queen beyond the third rank where she is prone to attack from the enemy minor pieces. Contravention of this maxim may result in loss of time occasioned by the queen having to seek sanctuary.

(c) Rook
The rooks should be united (i.e. one guarding the other) as soon as possible. Castling is a means of achieving this aim.

Rooks should be retained on the back rank, preferably on open files.

(d) Bishop
The bishops should be developed early in the game. The best squares for posting the white bishops (corresponding squares for the black bishop) are (1) c4/f4; (2) b5/g5 if pinning an enemy knight; (3) b2/g2 – the fianchetto; (4) d2/e2; (5) d3/e3 if here they do not block the advance of their respective centre pawns.

(e) Knight

Knights are employed to their best advantage in the opening. They should be developed towards the centre of the board unless there are good tactical reasons for not doing so.

(f) Pawn

The first thing to remember about the pawn move – and this applies to all stages of the game – is that, unlike the moves of other pieces, it may not be retraced. Therefore all pawn moves should be made only after careful deliberation. Ask yourself: "If I advance this pawn, am I likely to regret it later?"

A pawn advance on one or more of the four central files is normal and necessary in the opening. A single exception may be noted: f3 (f6) is almost invariably bad as it seriously weakens the king's position and takes away the best square for the king's knight.

A knight's pawn may be moved a single square to permit the development of a bishop; a rook's pawn a single square to prevent the pinning of a knight by a hostile bishop. But a good rule is: if in doubt, don't move a pawn.

2.   The Middle Game

(a) King

As in the opening, the king must be protected against attack. Towards the end of the middle game with most of the pieces off the board, an uncastled king which is required for active service is best advanced to the second rank rather than relegated to a wing position by the no-longer useful castling.

(b) Queen

The queen is a real power, and can often by manoeuvred to attack two undefended units simultaneously, thereby winning one of them. The queen should avoid picking up stray pawns if they beguile her from the scene of activities. On the other hand, a pawn safely won is a clear advantage.

This is a further point on which the expert can be

distinguished from the ordinary player – he knows which pawn can be safely captured and which pawn should be left alone.

(c) Rook
The rooks are best placed on the four centre files, particularly if any should be "open" (a file is said to be open if there are no friendly pawns on it). Doubled rooks (one behind the other) are very strong on an open file.

A rook (or better still, doubled rooks) on the seventh rank is something to be played for, as here the major pieces are immune from pawn attack, and assume the role of "cats among the pigeons".

Rooks are especially vulnerable to attack from the bishops – particularly if the latter are working in conjunction: therefore they should, if possible, be confined to the first two ranks unless an occupation of the seventh is feasible.

(d) Bishop
The bishops are the real workers – they never relax their activities throughout the game.

They are dangerous attacking pieces, but operate best like the rooks, from a distance where they are less open to attack themselves.

A common task of the bishop is to pin potentially active hostile knights.

As has been observed, the bishop, like the rook and the queen, operates to greater advantage on an open board.

The efficacy of the bishops depends on free diagonals, therefore avoid curtailing their range by obstructive pawn moves.

(e) Knight
Knights are quite at home in the middle game, and are best posted on advanced squares free from pawn attack.

They are economical in defence and very effective in attack.

Knights are least effective when guarding one another, since, if both are attacked by a piece, neither can move without loss of the other. They are most effective when working in conjunction on opposite-coloured squares.

(f) Pawn

The pawns are as important in the middle game as they are in the other stages.

In defence, they present a united front to direct onslaught; the more they are moved, the weaker they become as a body, creating "holes", or undefended squares, for occupation by enemy pieces.

In attack, the pawns are the battering-rams used to breach the enemy position. A spearhead of pawns, supported by pieces, advancing on a king position usually stands a greater chance of success than an attack by pieces alone.

Pawns are well-employed defending pieces from attack by hostile pieces, and they are also the best with which to attack hostile pieces because of their relatively inferior value.

It must be kept in mind throughout the middle game that all pawns are potential queens. Try to picture the skeleton when the meat is off, and play for a favourable end game position before forcing the exchange of too many pieces.

3.   The End Game

(a) King

In the ending, the king assumes the role of attacker, and his transitory function is to assist in pawn-promotion.

The versatility of the king at close range allows him to penetrate weak pawn structures.

Too often, when the end game is reached, players continue to manoeuvre their other pieces instead of bringing the kings forward.

If the opposing pieces are too strong, an early advance of the king is likely to prove an embarrassment.

(b) Queen
With the reduction in forces, the queen's power augments. If in a bad position in the middle game, the retention of the queen will at least offer chances of a "perpetual" in the ending, for a lone queen can sometimes force the draw in this manner.

(c) Rook
The rooks, since they are generally the last pieces to go into action in a game, are most commonly met with in end games; king, rook and pawns versus king, rook and pawns being by far the most frequent.

Several books have been written on the function of this piece in the ending alone, but briefly the work of the rook is confined to three fields:

1. Restricting the movements of the hostile king.
2. "Mopping up" and obstructing the advance of hostile pawns.
3. Protecting friendly pawns advancing to promotion.

A rook on the seventh rank – particularly if the enemy king is still on the eighth – is almost always strong, as in the middle game.

Two rooks on the seventh with the enemy king on the eighth usually draws by perpetual check against a similar piece-force, even if a pawn or two down.

Whereas an extra pawn in a king and pawn end game is usually sufficient to win, with rooks on the board there are more chances for a draw. Therefore if a pawn or more down in the ending, endeavour to retain a rook on the board.

All these factors should be borne in mind when the middle game is drawing to a close.

(d) Bishop
A paramount maxim to remember here is that if each side is left with a bishop and pawns, and the two bishops are on

opposite coloured squares, the game is often drawn, even if one side is a pawn or even two pawns ahead.

If a disadvantageous end game is foreshadowed, play to obtain bishops of opposite colours.

With bishops on squares of the same colour, however, even a small advantage on one side is often sufficient to win.

The reason for this is that, with bishops of opposite colours, the play of each side tends to be channelled onto the same colour squares as the respective bishops, leaving one party playing on the black squares and the other party operating on the white, thereby creating a deadlock. With bishops operating on the same coloured squares, force will be met by force, and an impasse is less likely to occur.

Another important fact to remember in the ending is that K, B and RP versus bare K is a draw where the bishop stands on a square the opposite colour to the pawn's promotion square; always provided that the solitary king can get in front of the advancing pawn. As in K and RP versus K, the superior force is compelled to surrender the pawn (leaving insufficient mating force) or give stalemate. With a bishop on the same-colour square as the promotion square, the stronger side always wins in this type of ending.

Bishops can be employed to good purpose preventing hostile pawn advances. For example, a white bishop on f1 prevents the advance of any black pawn in a chain of squares extending from f2 to e3, d4, c5 and b6. This is an elaborate case, but it demonstrates the power of the bishop in the end game.

If, in an ending, you are left with a bishop and pawns, the pawns should be advanced to squares of the *opposite* colour to that on which the bishop stands.

This may appear strange, since the bishop cannot then guard the pawns, but this drawback is outweighed by the bishop's greatly increased mobility, and the elimination of duplicated square control. It is quite a common sight to see a bishop reduced to the role of a pawn when the pieces stand on the squares of one colour.

(e) Knight
In the ending the powers of the knight are limited, owing to the comparative impotence of its march on a free board.

A player left with knight and pawns against a bishop and pawns should, if possible, force off by exchanges the pawns on one side of the board, as knight is seriously handicapped in having to watch both wings. The converse, of course, holds good – if left with a bishop and pawns against a knight and pawns, try to keep pawns on both wings, on which the bishop, with its greater powers, is able to operate simultaneously.

(f) Pawn
When we talk of the end game we are really discussing pawns, and their handling is therefore of the utmost importance.

Their play is examined at length in the chapter on the end game; it suffices here to quote a few general rules.

When there is a choice of pawn moves in the ending, the one that is farthest from the scene of operations (usually centred around the kings) should be made.

Remember always that a rook's pawn is insufficient to win, other things being equal, therefore pawn exchanges must be planned accordingly.

The advance of a pawn can be arrested by the sacrifice of a piece if necessary, a device which should not be overlooked.

In the ending, the remote wing pawns play their part, the centre struggle no longer dominating the game. A king cannot possibly stop two pawns, one advancing on each wing, but he can successfully blockade two centre pawns advancing together.

As with the other pieces, a cautionary eye must be kept on the pawns in the middle game, in order that they may be deployed to the best advantage when the final phase is reached.

Combinations
So much for the general manipulation of the pieces at the various stages. Let us now see how they can combine

effectively. The joint action of two or more pieces, working to achieve a desired object – to checkmate the opposing king, or capture material – is known as a combination; a sound combination if its purpose cannot be resisted, an unsound combination if there exists a plausible defence. Combinations are often initialized by a sacrifice.

There are a number of standard mates which keep occurring in one form or another, the dispersal of the majority of the pieces being purely incidental to the position.

A player should be able to recognize these positions at once, regardless of the camouflage concealing them.

The following examples are all quite common in practice, and cover many types of mating attack in the middle game. Be on guard against any and every similar position, however secure it may appear, for a deflective sacrifice, that cannot be declined, may be the prelude to catastrophe.

Mating Combinations

Example A (Diagram 15)

A variation of Fool's Mate, involving the sacrifice of a piece, is commonly encountered in play. It can occur in the opening: 1. f4 e5 2. fxe5 d6 3. exd6 Bxd6 4. Nc3? Qh4+ 5. g3 Qxg3+ 6. hxg3 Bxg3#.

Example B (Diagram 16)

A typical middle game sacrifice is to take the h-pawn with a bishop when the enemy king has castled on the king's side. A conclusive combination is often possible. In diagram 16 White wins by 1. Bxh7+ Kxh7? 2. Qh5+ Kg8 3. Ng5 Rfe8 4. Qh7+ Kf8 5. Qh8#.

Example C (Diagram 17)

After the sacrifice of a bishop for the h-pawn, the most common mating attack begins with the sacrifice of a bishop for the f-pawn against an unmoved king. Diagram 17 shows a typical example. White wins by 1. Bxf7+ Kxf7

DIAGRAM 15   **DIAGRAM 16**

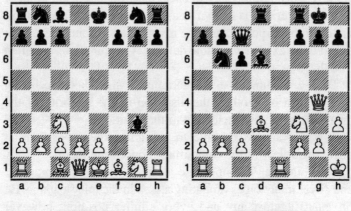

EXAMPLE A   EXAMPLE B

2. Ne5++ (that fearsome double check again! – the king must move) Ke6 (if 2. . . . Ke8 3. Qh5+ and mate in two; if 2. . . . Ke7 3. Ng6+ Ke6 4. Qg4#) 3. Qg4+ Kxe5 (again . . . Ke7 4. Ng6+) 4. Qf4+ Kd4 (or 4. . . . Ke6 5. Qf5+

DIAGRAM 17   **DIAGRAM 18**

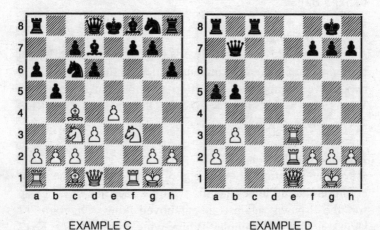

EXAMPLE C   EXAMPLE D

with mate to follow) 5. Be3#. The forced march of the black king into the centre of the board is a feature of this type of attack.

Example D (Diagram 18)
Mate on the back rank by a rook or the queen is common if the pawns in front of the king have not been moved. In diagram 18 White wins by: 1. Re8+ Rxe8 2. Rxe8+ Rxe8 3. Qxe8#. Always be alert to this possibility: decoy sacrifices are common.

Example E (Diagram 19)
An ingenious attack, involving a queen sacrifice on the penultimate move, is known as Philidor's Legacy, after a famous French player. White forces mate in five moves: 1. Qc4+ Kh8 (if 1. . . . Kf8 2. Qf7#) 2. Nf7+ Kg8 3. Nh6++ Kh8 (otherwise mate as above: note once again the power of the double check which White here uses to manoeuvre the knight to the desired square); 4. Qg8+ Rxg8 (the king cannot capture as the knight guards the queen) 5. Nf7#.

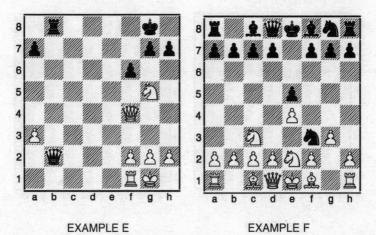

DIAGRAM 19   DIAGRAM 20

EXAMPLE E   EXAMPLE F

Example F (Diagram 20)

Philidor's Legacy demonstrates what is commonly known as a "smothered mate". The description is a good one; all the escape squares for the king being occupied by friendly(?) pieces who stifle the luckless monarch. Smothered mate can only be given by a knight, and is not uncommonly preceded by a sacrifice, as in the previous example. This device can occur in the opening: 1. e4 e5 2. Ne2 Nc6 3. Nbc3 Nd4 4. g3 Nf3#.

Example G (Diagram 21)

A position to be played for if your opponent has castled on the queen's side. White wins quickly by 1. Qxc6+ bxc6 2. Ba6#. Note the power of the two bishops working together.

Example H (Diagram 22)

A king behind a fianchettoed position from which the bishop has departed is very weak if the queens are still on the board, particularly if the other player has retained the bishop on the same coloured squares as the departed bishop, and/or a

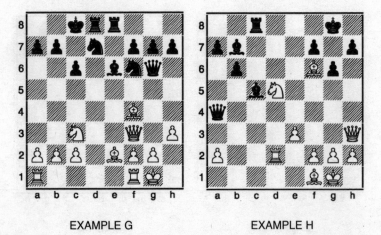

DIAGRAM 21   DIAGRAM 22

EXAMPLE G   EXAMPLE H

knight. Examples of this type are common, the strategy being to attack the weak squares in the king's field. In diagram 22 White wins by 1. Qh6 (threatening mate on the move) Bf8 2. Ne7+ Bxe7 3. Qg7#. In this type of position a pawn at f6 is often as good as a bishop; and with a queen established at h6, Nf6+ followed by Qxh7# is also a common finale.

Example I (Diagram 23)
A device against a fianchettoed position (normally difficult to attack). White mates in four by 1. Nf6+ Bxf6 2. Rxe8+ Kg7 3. Bf8+ K moves 4. Bh6#. If 1. . . . Kh8 2. Rxe8+ Bf8 3. Bxf8 and mates next move.

Example J (Diagram 24)
Another mating position often reached when the bishop has vacated the fianchetto. White mates in three by 1. Qxh7+ Kxh7 2. Rh3+ Kg8 3. Rh8#.

DIAGRAM 23   **DIAGRAM 24**

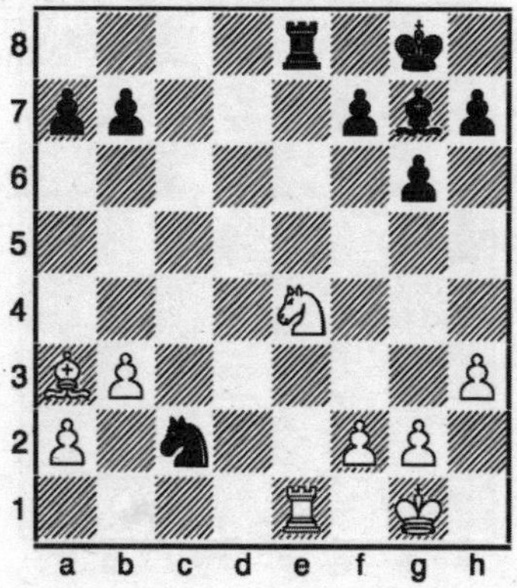

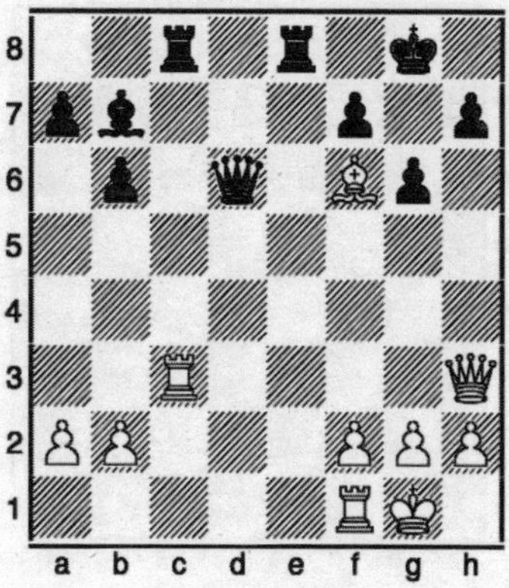

EXAMPLE I   EXAMPLE J

Example K (Diagram 25)
An end game attack on a castled king. White mates in three:
1. Re8+ Kh7 2. Bf5+ g6 3. Rh8#. The pawn move closes the
line of one bishop only to open a line for the other. All Black's
moves are forced.

Example L (Diagram 26)
With the hostile king in the corner, a typical mating set-up
starts with a queen sacrifice: 1. Qxh7+ Kxh7 2. Rh3#.

Example M (Diagram 27)
A less usual position, but nevertheless frequently occurring in
one form or another. White wins by 1. Rxg7+ Rxg7 2. Nf6+ Kh8
3. Qh5 and mate is unavoidable. If 1. . . . Kh8 White can win in a
number of ways, for example 2. Qg2 Be6 3. Qg6 and mate next
move. Black can prolong the agony by sacrificing the queen.

Material-Winning Combinations
There exist a number of typical combinations for winning
material (i.e. gaining an enemy piece or pieces for nothing,

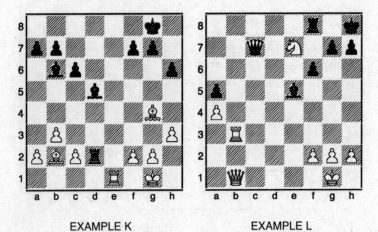

DIAGRAM 25   DIAGRAM 26

EXAMPLE K   EXAMPLE L

DIAGRAM 27

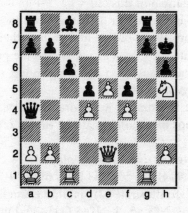

EXAMPLE M

or for the loss of a weaker piece) arising from certain positions that are met with time and again in one form or another.

A sound knowledge of these basic positions and how to exploit them will prove of inestimable value to the student.

Three good rules to observe in order to avoid loss of material are:

1. Watch all checks.
2. Watch all discovered checks.
3. Do not leave pieces undefended or insufficiently defended unless absolutely necessary.

Type A
An attack on the king (a check) may often succeed in winning material out of hand.

1. It may force the defender to interpose a stronger piece than the piece checking, which then captures it.
2. The checking piece may simultaneously attack an

undefended piece, or a more valuable piece (a knight fork is a good example of this).

3. The move may uncover an attack on another piece (a discovered attack).

4. If a piece on each side is attacked, and the player to move can evade the attack by a checking move, then the other piece, still *en prise*, will fall.

5. The skewer, illustrated in diagram 10, page 35, is yet another means of winning material in this fashion.

An example of (1) taken from play: 1. e4 c5 2. Nf3 d6 3. Nc3 Bg4 4. h3 Bxf3 5. Qxf3 Na6 6. Bb5+ and the queen must interpose. To illustrate (2), another example from actual play: 1. d3 c6 2. Nf3 e5 3. Nxe5 Qa5+ and the undefended knight is captured next move.

A trap in a well-known defence demonstrates the discovered attack (3): 1. e4 e6 2. d4 d5 3. e5 c5 4. c3 Nc6 5. Nf3 Qb6 6. Bd3 cxd4 7. cxd4 Nxd4 8. Nxd4 – the trap is sprung – 8. . . Qxd4? 9. Bb5+ and the black queen is lost (diagram 28).

A game opening will serve to make (4) clear: 1. e4 c5 2. Nf3 d6 3. Bc4 Bg4 4. Nc3 Nc6 5. h3 Bh5 6. g4 (attacking the bishop again) Na5 (attacking White's bishop) 7. Bb5+ winning a piece (diagram 29). These opening examples, given to demonstrate elementary strategy, are not, of course, intended as patterns of model play.

Type B
When two undefended pieces are attacked simultaneously, one is frequently lost. In diagram 30 the rook threatens both the knight and the bishop and must win one of them.

Type C – The Overworked Piece
A common failing of inexperienced players is to use one piece to perform two functions – for example, guarding two

DIAGRAM 28   DIAGRAM 29

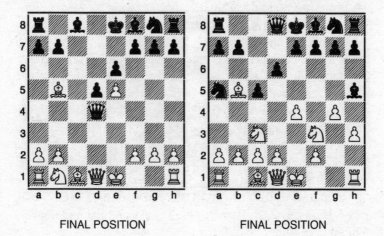

FINAL POSITION   FINAL POSITION

pieces. In diagram 31, the black king is defending both the knight and the bishop. White wins a piece by: 1. Nxa1 Kxa1 2. Kxc1.

Type D

Two knights guarding one another are weak. In diagram 32, the rook is attacking both knights. The white bishop is threatening to capture one of them, and Black must lose a piece.

DIAGRAM 30   DIAGRAM 31   DIAGRAM 32

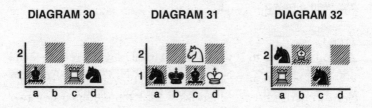

DIAGRAM 33

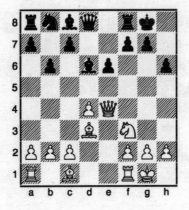

Type E

A similar type of manoeuvre to type A is the threat of mate combined with an attack on an undefended piece. Such a position may occur early in the game. Examine diagram 33, a position which can arise from an opening called the Colle System: Black has just exchanged on e4, which was bad because White now threatens both Qh7# and Qxa8. The mate must be attended to, and the rook is consequently lost.

Type F

The discovered attack often wins material: 1. e4 e5 2. Nf3 Nc6 3. Bc4 Nf6 4. d3 Nh5? 5. Nxe5 (discovering the queen attack on the unprotected knight) Nxe5 6. Qxh5 and White has won a pawn.

Type G

A similar device to F which also wins a pawn: 1. e4 e6 2. d4 d5 3. e5 c5 4. c3 Nc6 5. Bb5 Bd7 6. Nf3? Nxe5. And now if 7. Bxd7+ Nxd7 and if 7. Nxe5 (or dxe5) Bxb5.

DIAGRAM 34

This very common trap continues to net a large haul of victims (including quite experienced players) year after year. Diagram 34 gives the position after Black's sixth move.

Type H
A common material winning device, particularly in the opening, is the advance on a hemmed-in bishop: 1. e4 c5 2. Nf3 Nc6 3. Bc4 d6 4. 0-0 a6 5. Qe2 b5 6. Bd3? (likewise Bb3?, but White should prefer Bd5), c4 (diagram 35). White must give up the bishop for two pawns, an exchange we know to be unfavourable.

Type I
A pinned piece, being immobile, is particularly vulnerable to pawn attack. In the opening after, for example, 1. c4 e5 2. Nc3 Nc6 3. e3 Nf6 4. d4 d6 5. Qa4 Bf5? White wins a piece for a pawn by 6. d5 and Black's pinned knight must fall. Diagram 36 shows the position after White's final move.

DIAGRAM 35   **DIAGRAM 36**

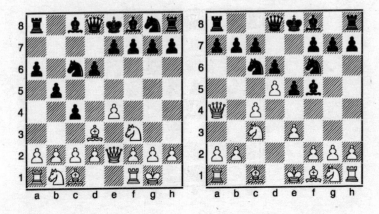

Type J

A king may be lured from the defence of a piece by a check – very often by a sacrifice. This is also liable to occur in the opening. A good example is offered: 1. e4 c5 2. Nf3 Nc6 3. d4 cxd4 4. Nxd4 Nf6 5. Nc3 d6 6. Bc4 g6 7. Nxc6 bxc6 8. e5 dxe5? 9. Bxf7+ (see diagram 37). Now Black must take with the king leaving the queen undefended.

Type K

A "forced" move, that is to say a move that must be made either to save the game or as a matter of legality, may frequently concede material. Diagram 38 shows a common stratagem. White plays here Bh6, threatening Qxg7#. The bishop cannot be taken as the g-pawn is pinned, and g5 would allow mate in two by Qxg5+, followed by Qg7. So g6 is forced, and now White wins the exchange by Bxf8.

DIAGRAM 37

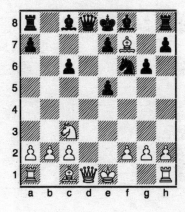

DIAGRAM 38

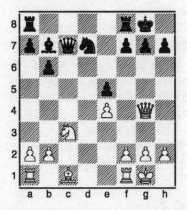

5

THE OPENINGS

Introduction

It has been seen that a game is divided arbitrarily into three phases: the opening, the middle game and the end game. An advantage gained in the opening will be carried into the middle game; so it follows that the opening will tend to shape the course of a game.

Chess openings have, as might be expected, provided the chief source of research for analysts down the ages. Fortunately no perfect opening has been discovered: the subtleties of a game invented by man transcend man's breadth of knowledge – and seem likely to do so for ever.

Nevertheless, chess scholars have succeeded in determining and classifying the best of the initial moves for both sides to various degrees of profundity. The net result of these years of constant research proves only that there is no proof; that if both players adopt the best lines of play, the game will remain approximately level. Theory is always changing – there are schools of thought in chess as in literature – and what was considered best a hundred years ago is classed as only mediocre today. Since analysis is recorded and published, however, the sum of our knowledge of the openings is constantly increasing – not a month passes without new discoveries, of greater or lesser importance, being added to this sum. Even a quite elementary book on the openings will bewilder the new player, conveying the impression that chess is a profound esoteric science rather than a game. Page upon page of continuations, prefaced by exotic names and punctuated with seemingly endless footnotes, each subdividing into further enumerated variations, are enough to frighten the most composed and self-confident of novitiates.

Such works, however, are rarely treated as more than sources of reference; mentors to indicate the pitfalls that attend the unwary, surgeons to assist the student conducting his own post mortem.

A good player will follow a book line without being conscious of doing so – simply because his moves are the best in the position with which he is confronted and, in consequence, are listed in the opening compendiums.

The purely "book" player, however, will be at a disadvantage if the opponent deviates from the accepted line. In order to play chess openings well, it is not only essential that an elementary knowledge of the approved lines is acquired, but, more important, that the ideas that activate these lines are clearly understood.

Openings are loosely divided into "open" and "close" games.

Open games are those in which the pieces are developed quickly, and the play is directed chiefly along tactical lines – games commencing: 1. e4 e5 are mostly in this category; close games are those in which play develops along strategical lines (for example: 1. d4 d5). Broadly speaking, pieces are posted *in front* of the pawns in open games, *behind* the pawns in close games. Certain openings fall between these two groups and are classed as "half-open".

There are about a score of important openings and several hundred minor and branch openings recognized. In each of these there are variations and sub-variations.

Some of these openings are acknowledged as better than others, but, in general, choice of opening is dependent upon style; players selecting lines of play (so far as it is in their power to do so) most suited to their temperament.

The majority of openings commence with: 1. e4 or d4. Occasionally one of the bishop's pawns is advanced, or a knight brought out first, but rarely a wing pawn. Openings that begin: 1. d4 – the close games – usually have deep-rooted ideas and involve long-term strategy, and are therefore best avoided in the early stages of a player's development. In this chapter attention will be mainly directed to those openings arising from: 1. e4.

All opening theory is based on the control of the centre, the importance of which has already been demonstrated. Control may be effected in three ways:

1. Occupation – by the establishment of pieces on the centre squares.
2. Delayed occupation – by permitting the opponent to occupy the centre at first, then attempting to undermine and break up the position.
3. Remote control – by commanding the centre from a distance by means of the pieces without actually occupying the squares. In this technique one or both bishops are fianchettoed.

Gambits

It is possible in the opening to sacrifice material in order to gain time in development. An opening sacrifice of this nature is called a gambit. There are a number of recognized gambits, the most common being the King's Gambit and the Queen's Gambit, in both of which a pawn is offered.

Amongst strong players, an extra pawn on one side in the opening, provided other factors – time and space, that together govern position – are equal, is usually sufficient to win.

With average club players of experience, a minor piece ahead will usually prove decisive. From this, it will be seen that a strong player who succeeds in refuting a gambit and obtaining equality in position is well on the way to victory.

Opening 1

After this superficial survey of opening theory, let us follow an established method of opening, endeavouring to understand the principles underlying the play. The reader may pass straight on to the next chapter, returning to the study of the openings after mastering middle and end game play.

White	Black
1. e4	e5

Black could also reply here 1 . . . . c5 (the Sicilian Defence); 1. . . . e6 (the French Defence); 1. . . . c6 (the Caro-Kann Defence); 1. . . . Nf6 (Alekhine's Defence); 1. . . . d5 (the Centre Counter or Scandinavian Defence), etc. This will give an idea of the choice open to the second player at the start of a game. Each of these defences has its own characteristics and its own advocates. After White's initial pawn advance, Black is in a position to dictate, to a great extent, the future course of the game.

2. Nf3	Nc6

We have already seen that both of these are good moves.

3. Bc4	Bc5

These three moves give the opening its name – the Giuoco Piano. The Giuoco is characterized by the quick development of the pieces and direct play in the centre. These straightforward aims recommend it to the student.

4. c3	

Preparing the advance of the d-pawn.

4. ...   **Nf6**

4. . . . Qe7 is a good alternative. Black's move attacks the undefended e-pawn.

5. d4   **exd4**
6. cxd4

The black bishop is again attacked, and since the d-pawn is twice protected, capture would only result in the loss of a piece. The white pawn on d4 is referred to as the d-pawn or the queen's pawn, even though it started life on c2. Pawns, unlike the other pieces, assume the name of the file on which they stand.

6. ...   **Bb4+**

A check to some purpose, as will be seen. No check should be made just for the pleasure of announcing it.

7. Bd2   **Bxd2+**
8. Nbxd2

Both white knights can capture the bishop, but this move develops another piece. Also, if 8. Nfxd2 Nxd4 and Black has won a pawn. If 8. Qxd2, Black replies Nxe4, again winning a pawn. 8. Kxd2 would be bad: (1) it would permit Black 8. . . . Nxe4+; (2) White would thereby surrender the privilege of castling; (3) the move would not help White's development.

8. ...   **d5!**

Black strikes at the right moment.

9. exd5   **Nxd5**

In open positions of this nature bishops are slightly superior

DIAGRAM 39

POSITION AFTER BLACK'S 11TH MOVE

to knights, so White prefers not to surrender the bishop with 10. Bxd5 Qxd5.

10. Qb3

Attacking the king's knight twice.

10. . . .   **Nce7**

Not 10. . . . king's knight moves 11. Bxf7+ nor 10. . . . Be6 11. Qxb7.

11. 0-0   **0-0**

Both sides castle king's-side and the position in diagram 39 is now reached. Black has equalized.

Opening 2
Another example of the Giuoco Piano, in which White gains the ascendency.

	White	*Black*
1.	e4	e5
2.	Nf3	Nc6
3.	Bc4	Bc5
4.	c3	Nf6
5.	d4	exd4
6.	cxd4	Bb4+

So far, the same as the previous example.

7. Nc3

White, instead of interposing the bishop (the more passive line), sacrifices a pawn for speedy development.

7. ...   Nxe4
8. 0-0

White is now threatening Nxe4. Note that before castling there was no threat as the queen's knight was pinned by the bishop.

8. ...   Bxc3
9. d5!

A surprising move. Instead of recapturing the bishop, White attacks another piece. Black has now two pieces attacked simultaneously by pawns, an undefended knight in a precarious position and a king in considerable danger. To compensate, Black is a piece and a pawn ahead.

9. ...   Ba5

9. . . . Bf6 was a sound alternative, which, according to theory, gives Black good chances.

DIAGRAM 40

POSITION AFTER WHITE'S 9TH MOVE

10. dxc6

White regains the piece and is now only a pawn in arrears.

10. . . .   **0-0?**

Black castles at the wrong moment. Correct was 10. . . . bxc6.

11. Qd5

A good example of when a queen may be brought out with safety in the opening. Black has two undefended pieces: the bishop on a5 and the knight. The queen now attacks them both.

11. . . .   **Nd6**

The only move. Black prepares a counter. If now 12. Qxa5 Nxc4.

12. Bd3

White now threatens to win a piece with Qxa5.

    12. . . .   **Bb6**
    13. Bxh7+

And here we are at the typical B/Q/N attack on the castled king (diagram 16, page 76). Black can only avoid mate by ruinous loss of material. A good sample of an open game: highly tactical, with time as valuable a commodity as force. In a close position, a player may make four or five consecutive moves with a knight in order to post it on a good square, whereas even two such moves in a game like this could result in calamity.

Opening 3

	White	Black
1.	e4	e5
2.	Nf3	Nc6
3.	Nc3	Nf6

Now all four knights are in play and the position is solid on both sides. This opening is known as the Four Knights' Game, and since it is lacking in punch – White's third move could hardly be called aggressive – it is favoured, in general, by those who like to "play safe".

4.	Bb5	Bb4
5.	0-0	0-0

The development of both sides has been logical. First the knights came out, then the freed bishops before the d-pawns were advanced to free the remaining bishops. Both sides then castled so that after the advance of the d-pawns, the queens' knights would not be pinned.

6. d3   **d6**
7. Bg5

Pinning the knight, White is threatening the powerful Nd5 putting further pressure on the pinned piece.

7. . . .   **Bxc3**
8. bxc3   **h6**

Attacking the bishop. Black cannot afford to release the knight by moving the queen, since White would then exchange bishop for knight when Black, being compelled to recapture with the g-pawn, would be left with a weak king's position. Often in the opening a knight can be unpinned by Qd6, a move which allows the recapture with the queen should the knight be taken. This move is not, of course, possible here as d6 is occupied by a pawn.

9. Bh4   **Qe7**

Black dare not now play g5 to release the knight, as the king's position would then become very weak. White could sacrifice with advantage: 10. Nxg5 hxg5 11. Bxg5, and the knight remains pinned with the black king deprived of all pawn shelter. Since Black did not intend to follow up the attack on the bishop, what was the point of h6? This type of position occurs in almost every opening and its anatomy is worth attention. The move does not lose time since the bishop is compelled to retire, and its importance lies in the fact that g5, although not immediately practical, can be held in reserve as an option should the need arise. Further, the move provides a square for the king at h7 which might prove useful later if back-rank mates threaten (see diagram 18, page 76).

10. Qd2

DIAGRAM 41

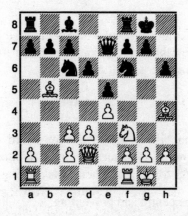

POSITION AFTER WHITE'S 10TH MOVE

A multi-purpose move. Its merits are worthy of analysis: (a) it prevents, at least for the time being, g5 since this would be swiftly punished: 10. . . . g5? 11. Nxg5 hxg5 12. Qxg5+ Kh7 13. Qxf6 and White stands two pawns to the good. (b) It neutralizes the counter-pin 10. . . . Bg4. (c) It unites the two white rooks, which we know to be desirable. (d) It affords protection to the undefended white pawn at c3.

The position in diagram 41 has now been reached. An assessment of the game at this point shows that White stands very marginally better: (a) the pin is still in place; (b) the b-file is open for the white rooks to occupy; (c) White has attack possibilities with an eventual advance of either the d- or f-pawn; (d) White has the slight advantage of the two bishops. Black is solid but has no visible attacking prospects at this stage.

Opening 4

The King's Gambit was very popular in the nineteenth century. The opening provides a good example of speedy development of the pieces; play is often wild with both sides in peril of a sudden collapse. Here is a typical skirmish:

	White	Black
1.	e4	e5
2.	f4	

This move establishes the opening. Black may now either accept or decline the gambit pawn.

2. ...	exf4

Black can decline the gambit by 2. . . . d5 or 2. . . . Bc5.

3. Nf3

Attacking the centre and preventing 3. . . . Qh4+. This early knight move is common to almost all openings and is very rarely inferior.

3. ...	g5

Black supports the pawn at f4. Notice that the g-pawn is guarded by the queen so White cannot play 4. Nxg5. The main point of White's play in the King's Gambit is the attack against the weak point in Black's defence: the f7 square. The surrender of the f-pawn by White opens the file for the rook (after castling) to bear indirectly against this weak point. In order to keep the f-file closed, Black endeavours to maintain the advanced pawn, but 3. . . . d6 is less hazardous.

4. h4

Hitting at the support.

4. ...	g4

Black has little option but to advance. If 4. . . . gxh4 Black's pawns are hopelessly weakened and neither f6 nor h6 is playable: (a) 4. . . . f6 5. Nxg5 fxg5 6. Qh5+ Ke7 7. Qxg5+

Nf6 8. e5 and White recovers the piece with a winning attack. Or (b) 4. ... h6 5. hxg5 hxg5 6. Rxh8 and wins.

5. Ng5

This variation is known as the Allgaier Gambit.

5. ...   h6

The knight is trapped.

6. Nxf7

White has sacrificed a piece to disrupt Black's king's side.

6. ...   Kxf7

Black has no choice as the rook and queen are forked.

7. d4

Now the bishop attacks the pawn on f4. Observe that White concentrates on speedy development. If 7. Qxg4 Nf6 and Black gains time by attacking the queen. 7. Bc4+ is also good.

7. ...   d5

Black must counter-attack quickly. 8. ... f3 was a good alternative.

8. Bxf4   Nf6

8. ... dxe4 allows 10. Bc4+, developing another piece. Black is aiming to keep the position as closed as possible. If the Black forces can be marshalled in time, the extra piece will prove a telling advantage.

9. Nc3

Black was threatening 10. ... Nxe4.

9. ...   Bb4
10. Be2

DIAGRAM 42

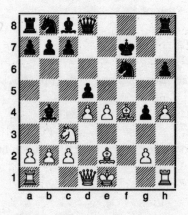

POSITION AFTER WHITE'S 10TH MOVE

White is staking everything on attack. The position now reached is typical of the opening; there are good chances for both sides in practical play, when there is the time factor to be considered (in fact, theoretically lost positions are often won in practice: time is on the side of the attacker). Notice that Black's queen's side is still undeveloped. (See diagram 42.)

Opening 5

One of the oldest and most popular openings is the Ruy Lopez, named after a Spanish priest of the sixteenth century. Recent analysis shows that the Lopez does not confer the marked advantage to White it was once thought it did, but no one will assert that the last work has been said on this remarkable opening.

The centre remains the focus of action for both sides, but strategy rather than tactics forms the basis of action.

	White	Black
1.	e4	e5
2.	Nf3	Nc6
3.	Bb5	

The purpose of this move is not at once apparent. It does not pin the black knight and the continuation 4. Bxc6 dxc6 5. Nxe5 is not a threat because of 5. . . . Qd4! attacking both the knight and the e-pawn, with a good game for Black.

3.	. . .	a6

Black attacks the bishop immediately with essentially the same idea we saw in Opening 3. Black has several playable moves in this position: 3. . . . Nf6; 3. . . . Bc5 and 3. . . . d6 are examples. The text (i.e. the move played) is probably the best, however, as after the retreat of the bishop Black may still adopt any of these continuations.

4.	Ba4	Nf6

Black develops a piece, attacking White's e-pawn in the process.

5.	0-0

White ignores the attack, sacrificing the pawn for speed of development.

5.	. . .	Nxe4

Black had the choice here of two contrasting lines of play. The text opens the game, promising lively play by both sides. The more popular alternative, 5. . . . Be7, keeps the position closed, at least for the time being. A good example of where players of different temperament and style would diverge.

6. d4

Vigorous play is called for.

| **6. ...** | **b5** |
| **7. Bb3** | **d5** |

Black counters in the centre and gives back the pawn. The player who accepts a sacrifice can often return the material at the right moment with advantage. The value of Black's third move is now clear. If it had not been played, White would have exchanged the bishop for the knight at the right time, hindering or even preventing the advance of Black's d-pawn.

8. dxe5

Nxe5 was also playable.

8. ....   **Be6**

White was threatening to capture the d-pawn.

9. c3

Securing the square d4 and allowing the king's bishop to be brought into play on the king's side.

9. ...   **Be7**

The main alternative is 9. . . Bc5, putting pressure on the
f2 square.

10. Nbd2	**0-0**
11. Qe2	

Threatening to win a pawn by 12. Nxe4 dxe4 13. Qxe4.

11. . . .	**Nc5**

A possible alternative is 11. . . . Nxd2, even though it
exchanges off a piece that has no immediate use and brings
White's bishop into play, thereby uniting the rooks.

12. Nd4

This move accomplishes several things. It stops the
advance of the d-pawn, attacks Black's knight, and allows the
f-pawn to advance with consequent gain in mobility for the

DIAGRAM 43

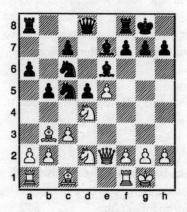

POSITION AFTER WHITE'S 12TH MOVE

rook behind it. The queen's knight now has a good square to move to, releasing the bishop. It is pleasing to see how positions unfold in this manner, each piece gracefully moving into its place in the opening framework.

This would be a good point to leave the game, which is on the point of entering the middle game stage. White is playing for a K-side attack, with the aim of keeping the centre and the queen's wing closed. Black, on the other hand, has no chances on the K-side, and will play for a Q-side attack. Note that Black has the pawn majority on the queen's wing, White on the king's wing, an alignment which is conducive to a two-wing struggle. In the position, Black's immediate aim is to play c5 as soon as possible – an objective which will be resisted by White. So long as the c-pawn remains backward, Black will be unable to assert superiority on this side. Broadly speaking, White may be said to have kept the advantage of the initial move.

Opening 6
The Queen's Gambit was first mentioned at the end of the fifteenth century but only gained popularity in the 1890s. In the 1920s and 1930s it became established as one of the most popular in tournament chess.

Compared with the King's Gambit, the Queen's Gambit is dull in the sense that there is little action in the initial stages. Both sides concentrate on developing their forces, which is accomplished without undue interference.

	White	*Black*
1.	d4	d5
2.	c4	

The Queen's Gambit. As in the King's Gambit, Black may now accept or decline the proffered pawn, but whereas in the King's Gambit acceptance of the pawn is normal, the reverse is true of the Queen's Gambit.

2. . . .   **e6**

This move shuts in the QB, the development of which is the chief headache for Black in this opening. Black can obviate the problem by playing here 2. . . . c6 (the Slav Defence), keeping the diagonal clear for the bishop, but it also has its disadvantages. If the Black d-pawn is left unattended, White gains time and a powerful centre with 3. cxd5 Qxd5 4. Nc3 followed by 5. e4.

3. Nc3   **Nf6**

White covets control of the two white squares in the centre, Black's move counters the attack.

4. Bg5

Pinning the knight, thereby neutralizing its restraining influence on the centre.

4. . . .   **Nbd7**

Setting a trap whilst developing a piece. If White now continues 5. cxd5 exd5 6. Nxd5? Nxd5! 7. Bxd8 Bb4+ 8. Qd2 (White has no option) Bxd2+ 9. Kxd2 Kxd8, Black has won a piece.

5. e3   **Be7**

White frees the king's bishop and also threatens cxd5 as now the king would have an escape square (e2) after the bishop check. Black's reply unpins the knight, and if now: 6. Bxf6 Nxf6 and not Bxf6, losing a pawn after 7. cxd5 exd5 8. Nxd5.

6. Nf3

A quiet developing move asserting White's control of e5.

| 6. ... | 0-0 |
| 7. Rc1 | |

The move order is important. The position is pregnant with possibilities, and as so often in chess, the most interesting variations are those which are not played.

| 7. ... | c6 |
| 8. Bd3 | dxc4 |

Black waits until after the bishop has moved before capturing the pawn, thereby causing White to lose time.

| 9. Bxc4 | Nd5 |

Black, whose pieces need air, must find a good square for the queen's bishop.

10. Bxe7	Qxe7
11. 0-0	Nxc3
12. Rxc3	e5

Black has at last succeeded in playing e5, freeing the bishop, but White is ahead in development.

13. dxe5

White decides to dissolve the centre.

13. ...	Nxe5
14. Nxe5	Qxe5
15. f4	

We now reach a position (diagram 44) commonly arrived at

DIAGRAM 44

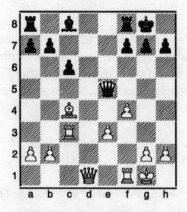

POSITION AFTER WHITE'S 15TH MOVE

in the Queen's Gambit. Although White has more pieces in play, Black's position is solid, and with correct play a draw should result.

Opening 7

We have seen that Black has several good defences to 1. e4 without replying 1. . . . e5; so too in answer to 1. d4, Black is not obliged to respond 1. . . d5 immediately. Popular is 1. . . . Nf6, which may lead into several defences. Here is the King's Indian Defence in which Black does not immediately challenge the centre.

	White	*Black*
1.	d4	Nf6
2.	c4	g6
3.	Nc3	Bg7

White prepares to take charge of the centre whilst the black bishop positions itself on the long diagonal.

4.	e4	d6
5.	f4	

The Four Pawns' Attack. This mass advance looks formidable but conversely it presents Black with a target. The advanced pawns are often difficult to defend and are thereby forced into further advances. 5. Nf3 is a more circumspect line for White.

5.	...	0-0
6.	Nf3	c5!

Striking at White's d-pawn. If 7. dxc5 Qa5 threatening Nxe4 and Black's development is excellent.

7.	d5	e6

A further undermining of the advance. If 8. dxe6 Bxe6 followed by Nc6. Black has a backward d-pawn but plenty of freedom.

8.	Be2	exd5
9.	cxd5	

Also playable is 9. exd5 when White relinquishes all idea of advancing the centre pawns.

9.	...	b5

Threatening 10. . . . . b4 followed by Nxe4 when the white knight moves, yet apparently losing a pawn for nothing. But after 10. Bxb5 Nxe4 11. Nxe4 Qa5+ 12. Kf2 Qxb5 13. Nxd6 Qa6 14. Nxc8 Rxc8 Black has a good game and value for the pawn lost with the white king dangerously exposed (diagram 45).

DIAGRAM 45

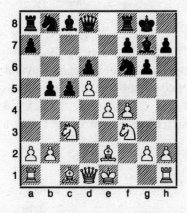

POSITION AFTER BLACK'S 9TH MOVE

Opening 8

In opening 1, several other defences to White's initial e4, other than e5, were mentioned. One of these, the Sicilian, is a very popular choice for the fighting player; it meets thrust with thrust and counter-thrust with counter-thrust.

	White	*Black*
1.	e4	c5

Threatening to take off the d-pawn should it advance.

2.	Nf3	d6
3.	d4	cxd4
4.	Nxd4	Nf6
5.	Nc3	g6

Black prepares to fianchetto the king's bishop – the Dragon variation.

6.	Be2	Bg7
7.	Be3	Nc6
8.	0-0	0-0
9.	Nb3	Be6

Both sides are now preparing to attack, White on the king's side (notice the two bishops and the f-pawn poised for assault) and Black on the queen's side (Black's king's bishop, although screened, is trained on White's rook at a1).

10. f4

Attack!

10. . . .   **Na5**

Counter-attack!

11.	f5	Bc4
12.	Nxa5	Bxe2

Not of course 12. . . . Qxa5 13. Bxc4.

13.	Qxe2	Qxa5
14.	g4	

White flings caution to the winds. Should the attack fail and the majority of the pieces stay on the board, White's king will be difficult to defend. A safer alternative was 14. Bd4.

14. . . .   **Nd7**

Perhaps a better option was 14. . . . Rac8, planning to sacrifice the exchange on c3.

15. Nd5

DIAGRAM 46

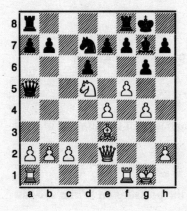

POSITION AFTER WHITE'S 15TH MOVE

So far, White has had most of the game and has a slight advantage in position, but Black has plenty of fight and, if White pauses, a reversal of fortunes is likely. It is on this razor-blade margin between success and failure that the appeal of the opening rests.

Opening 9

The French Defence is an ideal opening for the patient player. Black allows White to build up a strong pawn centre and then harasses it from the flanks. As in the Queen's Gambit, Black's chief worry is the development of the queen's bishop which is imprisoned by the very first move.

	White	*Black*
1.	e4	e6

It is this move that gives the opening its name.

2.	d4	d5

The almost invariable second moves.

3. e5

This advance is often delayed.

3. ...   **c5**

Hitting immediately at the support of the e-pawn.

4. c3   **Nc6**

Keeping up the pressure on White's d-pawn.

5. Nf3   **Qb6**
6. Be2   **cxd4**
7. cxd4   **Nge7**
8. b3

White could also develop his queen's knight here.

8. ...   **Nf5**

Black brings the second knight to bear on the d-pawn which
has now been deprived of its pawn support.

9. Bb2   **Bb4+**
10. Kf1

The only move, for if a piece is interposed the d-pawn
falls. An assessment of the position (diagram 47) reveals that
White has so far maintained the pawn at e5, a powerful
wedge in the centre. Black, however, still has three pieces
trained on the weak d-pawn and has prevented White from
castling whilst retaining a solid defence position. A factor in
favour of White, and by no means obvious, is the mutual

DIAGRAM 47

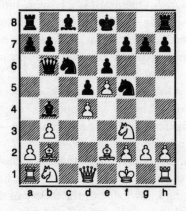

POSITION AFTER WHITE'S 10TH MOVE

interference of the black bishop at b4 and the knight at f5. Both can be attacked by pawns and both would then best be placed at e7. White will now bring the king to g2 after advancing the g-pawn and may attack with almost equal facility on either side. Black will rely for defence on a sound position and the pressure on the d-pawn. Note that Black's game is cramped and that the bishop at c8 is still undeveloped – two typical features of the French.

Summary

The examples given above are not arranged in any kind of order but they are generally representative of their respective openings and run the gamut from the patently aggressive (King's Gambit) to the stolidly defensive (French Defence).

But how, the reader asks, am I to assimilate a seemingly endless string of variations, where the first slip may prove dangerous if not fatal?

Fortunately there is no need to learn more than one or two

openings. For example, with the white pieces you will be able to play the English Opening (1. c4) with little fear of your opponent transposing it into another. As Black, in reply to 1. e4, the French, Sicilian or Caro-Kann are three good resources at your disposal, and you can specialize in one of these. After 1. d4, the Dutch Defence (1. . . . f5) is a way of circumventing a lot of opening theory.

If, on the other hand, you open 1. e4 yourself, your opponent will be able to choose a pet defence – a factor which will offset the advantage of the move.

However, the adoption of selective lines, based on personal preference of style should be left until you have acquired a thorough working knowledge of the theory of the game. Until you are reasonably sure of yourself, the advice offered earlier still applies: 1. e4 is the best opening move.

It is said that you cannot ride a horse properly until you have been thrown a few times. The same holds good for chess; more being learned from a few opening débâcles than this, or any other chapter could impart.

Major Openings

A short list of the openings commonly met with is given below in alphabetical order. In each example, try to visualize the central pawn structure, the development of the pieces and the strategical aims of each side. It sometimes happens that one opening transposes into another (for example, a Petroff becomes a Four Knights'). Artful transpositions have become a technique of modern master play.

Albin Counter-Gambit (1. d4 d5 2. c4, *e5* followed after 3. dxe5 by 3. . . . d4). Black surrenders a pawn for the sake of quick development. Generally good for White.

Alekhine's Defence (1. e4 *Nf6*). Black entices the white pawns to advance by offering the king's knight as a target. Normally slightly favourable to White.

Benko Gambit (1. d4 Nf6 2. c4 c5 3. d5 *b5*). A modern gambit which White usually accepts.

Benoni (1. d4 *c5*). A relatively recent addition to Black's repertoire, more often seen in the form of the Modern Benoni (1. d4 Nf6 2. c4, c5).

Bird's Opening (1. *f4*). An opening which will resemble a Dutch Defence with a move in hand if Black replies with 1. . . . d5.

Bishop's Opening (1. e4 e5 2. *Bc4*). Can transpose into other openings such as the Giuoco Piano.

Budapest Defence (1. d4 Nf6 2. c4 *e5*). Black surrenders a pawn for a quick counter-attack. White usually gains a slight advantage if he avoids the resulting pitfalls.

Caro-Kann Defence (1. e4 *c6*). A popular defence to the king's pawn, the Caro-Kann is sound but unambitious. It avoids the drawback of the French – shutting in of the queen's bishop – but has other problems. Slightly favourable to White.

Catalan Opening (1. d4 d5 2. c4 e6 3. *g3*). A relation of the Queen's Gambit in which White fianchettoes his king's bishop. Various move orders are possible.

Centre Game (1. e4 e5 2. *d4*). White relies on the initiative and breaks open the centre at once. Equal chances.

Colle System (1. d4 d5 2. Nf3 Nf6 3. *e3*). A solid queen's pawn game in which White develops quietly, aiming to play e4 later on. Black should be able to gain easy equality.

Danish Gambit (1. e4 e5 2. d4 exd4 3. *c3*). Followed, after 3. . . . dxc3 by 4. Bc4 cxb2 5. Bxb2. An offshoot of the Centre Game, the Danish gives White good chances in practice, at least at lower levels, despite the loss of the two gambit pawns, due to the free development obtained for the pieces.

Dutch Defence (1. d4 *f5*). Black aims at controlling e4. The game is usually close in the early stages. White has slightly the better of it as a rule.

English Opening (1. *c4*). In this opening, the fianchetto of the king's bishop is normal for the first player. White is often playing the Sicilian Defence with a move in hand but Black has several good lines.

Evans Gambit (1. e4 e5 2. Nf3 Nc6 3. Bc4 Bc5 4. *b4*). The Evans offers White many compensations for the pawn; a strong centre, quick development and good attacking chances. The safest option, as is often the case with gambits, is for Black to give the pawn back at the right moment.

Four Knights' Game (1. e4 e5 2. Nf3 Nc6 3. Nc3 *Nf6*). A solid opening giving little advantage to the first player.

French Defence (1. e4 *e6*). A common reply to e4. Both players now advance their queens' pawns when Black has a secure but rather restricted position. Popular with positional players who are content to work for an end game advantage. White usually plays for a king's side attack.

Giuoco Piano (1. e4 e5 2. Nf3 Nc6 3. Bc4 *Bc5*). A very old opening. Sharp attacks by either side are not uncommon. Equal game.

Grünfeld Defence (1. d4 Nf6 2. c4 g6 3. Nc3 *d5*). After the usual 4. cxd5 Nxd5 5. e4 Nxc3 6. bxc3, Black aims to exploit the a1 – h8 diagonal on which White is weak.

King's Gambit (1. e4 e5 2. *f4*). Once one of the most popular openings, the King's Gambit is now played less often as White's second move is considered too loosening. The gambit is the starting point of many adventurous lines: the Allgaier, Bishop's Gambit, Kieseritzky, and Muzio are examples. The pawn offer may either be declined or accepted. In either case, Black has equal chances with correct play. The opening is highly tactical.

King's Indian Attack. An opening in which White plays the moves Black commonly plays in the King's Indian Defence (Nf3, g3, Bg2, d3, Nbd2, e4). Numerous move orders are possible.

King's Indian Defence (1. d4 Nf6 2. c4 g6 3. Nc3 *Bg7*). Now one of the most popular defences, giving Black good chances. White usually adopts one of two general systems: a large pawn centre with the king's bishop posted at e2 or d3, or a less ambitious pawn advance with the bishop posted at g2. Black sometimes has difficulty in finding good squares for the minor pieces. Other openings such as the English and Réti can often transpose into the King's Indian.

Modern Defence (1. e4 g6 2. d4 *Bg7*). A close relation of the Pirc and King's Indian Defences. Black opens with a king's side fianchetto and will later attack White's centre with c5 or e5.

Nimzo-Indian Defence (1. d4 Nf6 2. c4 e6 3. Nc3 *Bb4*). A popular and versatile defence, described at the equivalent of the Ruy Lopez in the Queen's Pawn Game (q.v.). A game of strategic possibilities.

Nimzo-Larsen Attack (1. *b3*). As with most flank openings, White plans to control the centre by indirect play. Black should have no difficulty in equalizing.

Petroff's Defence (1. e4 e5   2. Nf3 *Nf6*). Black counter-attacks at once. A sound reply to 1. e4, usually good for a draw with best play.

Philidor's Defence (1. e4 e5 2. Nf3 *d6*). White gets the more mobile game as Black's king's bishop is shut in.

Pirc (1. e4 d6 2. d4 *Nf6*). A resilient but rather passive defence.

Queen's Gambit Accepted (1. d4 d5 2. c4 *dxc4*). Black takes the gambit pawn, intending to return it later rather than hold onto it. This usually leads to more lively play than declining the gambit.

Queen's Gambit Declined (1. d4 d5 2. c4 *e6*). This has been one of the most popular openings for more than a century, reaching the peak of its popularity in the 1920s and 1930s. Black achieves a solid position at the cost of hemming in his queen's bishop.

Queen's Indian Defence (1. d4 Nf6 2. c4 e6 3. Nf3 b6 4. g3 *Bb7*). Black aims to control e4 and prevent the advance of White's e-pawn. White prepares to face bishops on the diagonal.

Réti Opening (1. *Nf3*). Coupled with c4, g3 and Bg2, the aim is control of the centre without occupation in the hope that Black will set up a rigid pawn structure that will then be vulnerable to attack. A typical flank opening.

Ruy Lopez (1. e4 e5 2. Nf3 Nc6 3. *Bb5*). One of the oldest and most popular of openings, the Ruy abounds in complex strategical ideas in which the stronger player is likely to come out on top.

Scandinavian Defence or Centre Counter (1. e4 *d5*). Black immediately counters in the centre. Vigorous play, normally with some advantage to White.

Scotch (1. e4 e5   2. Nf3 Nc6   3. *d4*). After 3. . . . exd4 4. Nxd4, the Scotch Game, there are few terrors for the second player. White can instead give up the pawn with 4. Bc4, the Scotch Gambit, but Black should have no difficulty in withstanding the attack.

Sicilian Defence (1. e4 *c5*). Nowadays the most popular defence to 1. e4. Generally, White plays an early d4 where-upon Black exchanges pawns. Black then attempts to play d5 when it is safe to do so. Débâcles in this opening are not uncommon but results are evenly balanced.

Slav Defence (1. d4 d5   2. c4 *c6*), also the Semi-Slav (1. d4 d5   2. c4 c6   3. Nc3 *e6*). A resourceful and interesting defence to the Queen's Gambit. The Meran System (which either side can avoid) is an exciting variant of the Semi-Slav offering equal chances.

Trompowsky Opening (1. d4 Nf6   2. *Bg5*). An increasingly popular way for White to avoid theory. Usually leads to an equal game.

Two Knights' Defence (1. e4 e5   2. Nf3 Nc6   3. Bc4 *Nf6*). An alternative to the Giuoco Piano 3. . . . Bc5. Interesting play follows 4. Ng5 attacking the weak f-pawn. On the whole, chances are about even.

Vienna (1. e4 e5   2. *Nc3*). Gives a fairly equal game. After 2. . . . Nc6   3. f4, we have the Vienna Gambit, not dissimilar to the King's Gambit.

6

THE MIDDLE GAME

Introduction
In the opening and the end game the chess player can fall back to a considerable extent on the labour of others.

In the middle game, however, you are on your own.

Very little clear-cut instruction can be given on this phase of the game, but there exists an extensive field of theory. A lot of this theory is based on personal preferences, but certain aims, and the means of achieving these aims, are endorsed by all authorities. It is with this field of accepted theory that we are concerned in this chapter.

The Importance of the Centre
A lot has been said already on the subject. Pawns and pieces established on, or controlling, centre squares also exert their influence on both wings.

Most pieces, we know, have greater scope when in the middle of the board. A knight posted on a central square can be transferred to any position in two or three moves whereas a knight on the edge of the board would require several moves to reach a vital point on the other wing.

As in warfare, the breakthrough in the middle is the most effective, the defence forces being split into two camps which, being to a degree interdependent, are the more easily destroyed.

A wing attack, even if successful, may not be decisive. In practice, however, the wing attack is the more common because, as a result of the necessity of central concentration in the early stages of the game, a deadlock is frequent here.

Piece Exchanges

The vexed question of when and when not to exchange has been long encumbered by prejudice.

Be guided only by the position; if you are ahead in material, endeavour to force exchanges and so increase your strength ratio; if behind, avoid exchanges, particularly of queens, and remember that endings with bishops of opposite colours are very often drawn. Do not let favouritism affect your judgement: many otherwise good players admit to preferences for this or that piece and avoid exchanging even when to do so would be to their advantage.

Ask yourself the following questions when contemplating an exchange:

1. Am I ahead in material and well placed for the end game?
2. Which of the two pieces, mine or my opponent's, is the stronger or likely to become the stronger?
3. Am I losing time by taking his piece off, and would it not be better to let mine be taken first?

Let the answers determine your course of action.

Pawns and Pawn Structures

The importance of the pawn structure is difficult to over-estimate. Pawns can be battering-rams for the attack, bulwarks for the defence; and they can also be grave liabilities in either.

Because of the great influence that pawn formations exert on the middle game, and to a lesser degree on the opening and end game, a comprehensive survey of their diverse functions and their merits and demerits is given. Again, generalization has been necessary, and the relative position of the pieces, material and temporal factors must also be taken into account.

Isolated Pawn
A pawn is isolated if there is no friendly pawn on either of the two adjacent files. Because it cannot receive pawn support, an isolated pawn is weak.

Doubled Pawns
Pawns are said to be doubled if there are two of the same colour on a file. Doubled pawns are unable to support each other and are particularly vulnerable to attack. Their value is relatively slight (one pawn is able to block two hostile pawns that are doubled). Doubled, isolated pawns are weaker still. Occasionally pawns may be trebled or even quadrupled on a file. Sometimes, however, doubled pawns can provide extra central control or open a file for a rook.

Passed Pawn
A passed pawn is one which is faced with no hostile pawn either on the same file or on one of the two adjacent files.

A passed pawn is a distinct asset, particularly in the ending, since it will command the attention of an enemy piece to restrain its advance.

Backward Pawn
A backward pawn, as its name implies, is a pawn that has been "left behind" and thereby deprived of its pawn support. It is weak because to all intents and purposes it is isolated. A

DIAGRAM 48

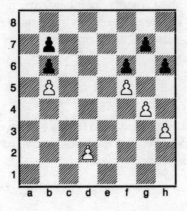

backward pawn on a half-open file (a file with no enemy pawns) is particularly vulnerable to attack.

United Pawns

Pawns standing side by side or supporting one another are said to be united. United pawns are strong.

Diagram 48 gives examples of the pawn types mentioned. The white pawns on b5 and d2 are isolated. The two black pawns on b6 and b7 are doubled and isolated. They are blocked by the single white pawn.

The white pawn on d2 is a passed pawn, notwithstanding that it has not yet moved and is isolated. Black's pawn at g7 is backward; it cannot advance without being captured by the white pawn at f5. Both the pawn formations on the king's side are composed of united pawns.

Pawn Formations

A pawn formation is a series of united pawns; it may be mobile or static in character.

DIAGRAM 49

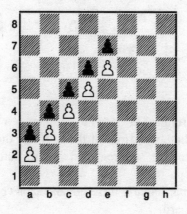

(a) **Mobile.** The strongest mobile formation is line abreast, provided the pawns have ample piece support.

(b) **Static.** The strongest static pawn formation is one in the form of a wedge with the apex in the centre, or a single diagonal chain directed towards the centre. A chain extending outwards from the centre of the board is weak. Diagram 49 will make this clear. The White pawn structure is strong, that of Black weak. White controls by far the greater space. The structure is static (none of the pawns can move) and the play would therefore be confined to the pieces. Such formations are uncommon; but chains of three pawns, as in the last diagram, occur in many games at one stage or another.

United Pawn Structures

Structures of three united pawns are very common, and every combination, together with general remarks on the intrinsic value of each, is given below. For combinations of four or more pawns, the assessment has only to be extended. Orientations and reflections of a basic structure are not included.

DIAGRAM 50　　　**DIAGRAM 51**　　　**DIAGRAM 52**

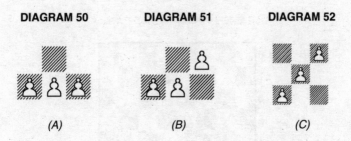

(A)　　　　　　　*(B)*　　　　　　　*(C)*

(A) Very strong. The pawns command a line of five squares immediately in front of them. If any one is attacked, it may advance one square when it will automatically be defended.

(B) Strong, particularly if the advanced pawn is nearest the centre of the board.

(C) Strong if the apex is towards the centre, weak if away from the centre. Any bishops remaining on the board must also be taken into account. If White has a bishop on the opposite colour to that on which the pawns stand, their value is enhanced; on the other hand, if Black has a bishop on the opposite colour, it will diminish the value of the structure. The reason for this has already been explained in Chapter 4.

DIAGRAM 53　　　**DIAGRAM 54**　　　**DIAGRAM 55**

(D)　　　　　　　*(E*　　　　　　　*(F)*

(D) Strong if combined with a bishop on the opposite colour.

(E) Moderately strong if the backward pawn is nearest to the edge of the board, weaker if nearest the middle.

(F) Generally weak, but, if the centre pawn can be advanced, will be strong. The "hole" is an ideal post for a hostile piece.

DIAGRAM 56   **DIAGRAM 57**

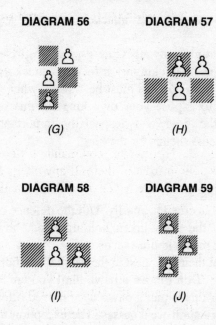

(G)   (H)

DIAGRAM 58   **DIAGRAM 59**

(I)   (J)

(G) Weak, particularly if there is a single black pawn in front of the foremost white pawn.

(H) Weak, but slightly better if the double pawn is away from the centre.

(I) Weak, but not so weak as *(G)* or *(H)*.

(J) Very weak. Again the question of the opposite-coloured bishops will arise.

Pawns in Attack

Supposing Black has castled on the king's side, and the moment is propitious for attack, which pawn or pawns should White advance?

The choice usually falls between the f-pawn and the h-pawn. It must be remembered that pawns are easily blocked by opposing pawns. But a defender will often be compelled to weaken the attacker to make a profitable sacrifice.

White sometimes advances the g-pawn to drive away an enemy piece (usually a knight) at f6, or to attack a pawn that has been played to h6. You must be careful, when advancing like this, not to expose your own king. In this respect the advance of the g-pawn is especially important since it provides the most shelter for the king.

Pawns in Defence

Here we are concerned primarily with the defence of the king after castling, the rules given holding good, however, for defence under most circumstances.

Pawns are at their strongest in their initial positions, and the golden rule is: "Don't move a pawn until you are forced to." The reason for this is that a pawn once moved offers a target and creates structural weaknesses. The exception to this rule is a pawn advance to the third rank in order to fianchetto a bishop.

The defence of the castled king depends to a large extent on the make-up of the attacking forces. Supposing White, who has castled king's side, is under fire from Black. The most vulnerable point is h2 (compared to f2 prior to castling), particularly if Black has retained the king's bishop. White must be careful of the move h3 if Black's queen's bishop is still on the board, for the sacrifice Bxh3 is a common way to break open the king's position since, after gxh3, the king is stripped bare.

The main pawn positions that can arise in front of a castled king, together with remarks on the strong and weak points of each, are given in outline:

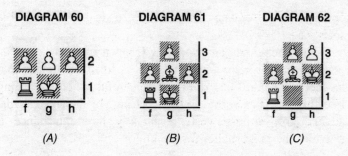

DIAGRAM 60   **DIAGRAM 61**   **DIAGRAM 62**

(A)   (B)   (C)

(A) Strong; particularly if there is a knight at f3 to guard the h-pawn.

(B) Strong; particularly if Black has not the same coloured bishop.

(C) Quite strong; but not so favourable as the first two. Vulnerable to pawn attack.

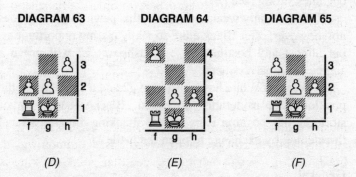

DIAGRAM 63   **DIAGRAM 64**   **DIAGRAM 65**

(D)   (E)   (F)

(D) Quite strong if there is also a knight at f3. May be dangerous if Black has retained the bishop that can attack the h-pawn, or if Black is able to advance the g-pawn with impunity.

(E) Strong; particularly if a knight can be brought to f3.

(F) Weak, but not unduly so, particularly if f4 can be played in safety.

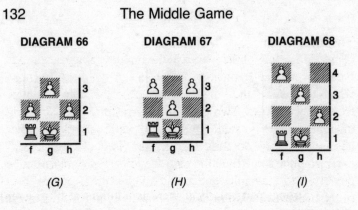

DIAGRAM 66   DIAGRAM 67   DIAGRAM 68

(G)   *(H)*   *(I)*

(G) Very weak if the black queen is on the board supported by one or more of the following: (1) Queen's bishop; (2) One or both knights; (3) A pawn that can be established at f3 or h3 (i.e. either of the holes formed by the advance of the g-pawn). As has been seen in Chapter 4, it is not difficult to mate a king in this position. Of course, if the white king's bishop is still on the board and can be brought to g2, the position immediately becomes strong (see *(B)*).

(H) Structurally weaker than *(G)*, this pawn formation does not, however, offer Black quite so many mating opportunities, but almost any hostile man established at g3 will prove a source of embarrassment.

(I) Weak. If White has a bishop at g2 and a knight at f3, the position is considerably improved. Black's best way of storming this position is by h5 h4, attacking the g-pawn and threatening by exchange to open the h-file.

General

All other pawn formations in front of a castled king are bad; if the rook has been moved away, each position is proportionately worse. The criterion in all the examples, and in *(G)* and *(H)* in particular, lies in whether Black has adequate force and is sufficiently well placed to carry out an attack. If the end game is reached, the pawn structure, so far as the defence of the king is concerned, is inconsequential.

The Pieces

General handling of the pieces in the middle game has already been covered. The bishops and rooks need open lines on which to operate; the knights strong central squares immune from pawn attack. Two bishops co-operate well, covering diagonals side by side. Queen and knight work together harmoniously, as do rook and bishop. Two or more pieces exercising the same function on a file, diagonal or rank can be powerful; for example, queen and bishop (the queen in front of the bishop) attacking a square, especially in the field of the enemy king. Also two rooks, rook and queen or two rooks and queen on a file or rank (the queen behind the rook(s) here). As far as the ranks go, the seventh and occasionally the eighth are the only two that come in for consideration, as on these the major pieces are secure from pawn attack.

Strong and Weak Squares

Every move by either side may result in a change of square values. A weak square may be said to be a hole in the pawn formation – the result, in the majority of cases, of a backward pawn. This weak square will be a strong point for the other side, and since, by definition, it is immune from pawn attack, it will be an ideal post for a piece. Weak squares may be only temporarily weak, however. The creation and exploitation of weaknesses is one of the fundamentals of master chess.

Open and Close Positions

Blocked positions are not common in chess, although one wing may become paralysed as the result of the rival pawn formations interlocking.

If it is intended to attack on one side of the board, it is often advisable to seal the other side in order to forestall any possible counter-attack in that quarter. This can be accomplished by timely pawn advances.

In a close position, in particular, the ultimate pawn skeleton should be considered with regard to the end game. Open positions are often decided by direct attack in the middle game, and here precise calculation is paramount.

In open games, which can arise from close openings it should be noted, the prestige of the pawn suffers; but often exchanges result in some neglected pawn proving the decisive factor.

Piece Traps

There are several traps for winning material that are perennial. It is consequently well worthwhile to commit them to memory. (The examples given are *basic* structures which must be recognized in game settings and are not, of course, game positions complete in themselves.)

(A) **Knight**. Be careful to leave an escape square for a knight after playing it to the side of the board, otherwise the advance of a hostile pawn may win it. The same care should be taken if a knight is on the fifth rank with an enemy pawn behind controlling the two best escape squares.

Example: (i) WHITE: N on h4, Ps on e5, f2, g2; BLACK: Ps on e6, g7, h7. If White plays 1. f3?, Black wins the knight by 1. . . . g5.

(ii) WHITE: N on e5, Ps on d4, e3, f4; BLACK: K on e8, N on e7, Ps on d5, e4, f7, h5. Black wins the knight by 1. . . . f6.

(B) **Bishop**. The trapping of a bishop by pawns was demonstrated in Chapter 4. Another common device is the shutting in of a bishop that captures an undefended rook's pawn.

Example: WHITE: B on e3; BLACK: R on c8, Ps on a7, b7, c7. If White now takes the pawn – 1. Bxa7, Black plays 1. . . . b6, closing the bishop's escape route and threatening Ra8 and Rxa7.

(C) **Rook**. A bishop is sometimes able to shut in a rook, winning the exchange.

Example: WHITE: R on e4, P on a2; BLACK: B on d6, Ps on a5, b7. If White now attacks the a-pawn, disaster awaits:

1. Ra4? Bb4 (now the rook cannot escape) 2. a3 b5, winning the exchange for a pawn.

(D) **Queen**. A queen can be trapped if she ventures too far into enemy territory, particularly if she has only one line of retreat.

Example: WHITE: Q on a1; BLACK: K on c7, R on d8, B on b7, Ps on a7, b6. If 1. Qxa7? Ra8 and the queen cannot escape.

The Seventh Rank

In Chapter 4 we remarked on the power of the rook on the seventh rank and we also investigated the potentialities of the discovered check. A type of position not by any means uncommon illustrates the devastating effect of the combination of these two forces: WHITE: R on e7, B on a1: BLACK: K on g8, Q on a8, Ns on d7, f8, Ps on a7, b7, c7, g7. Here the black queen, apparently secure in the corner, falls along with all of Black's queen's side men; 1. Rxg7+! Kh8 (the only square) 2. Rxd7+(discovered check) Kg8   3. Rg7+ Kh8 4. Rxc7+ (discovered check) Kg8   5. Rg7+ Kh8   6. Rxb7+ (discovered check) Kg8   7. Rg7+ Kh8   8. Rxa7+ (discovered check) Kg8   9. Rxa8.

General Maxims

Before going on to practical examples of middle game play, a few general maxims will not come amiss.

(a) Watch for forks. To someone not familiar with the moves of the pieces, the fork is a perpetual source of worry, particularly where knights are concerned. Even experienced players frequently overlook queen forks, which, because queens are long-range pieces, are often difficult to see. But all pieces are able to fork, and you should keep tactical as well as strategic considerations in mind at all times.

(b) Watch the back rank. Even if no immediate danger threatens, a "hole" for the king by moving up a pawn is always a sound investment if time and position permit.

(c) Do not attack undefended pieces for the privilege of driving them to better squares. Such pieces are best left "hanging" as they may become ideal targets for combinations at a later stage.

(d) After castling K-side, be careful of advancing the f-pawn if the hostile king's bishop can check. There is a prosaic finesse winning the exchange which is common to such positions:

WHITE: K on g1, Q on d1, R on f1, Ps on f4, g2, h2; BLACK: B on e7, N on g4 or e4. White has just played 1. f4? Play now runs 1. . . . Bc5+ 2. Kh1 Nf2+ (forking king and queen) 3. Rxf2 Bxf2. Black has won a rook for a bishop.

(e) Do not bring rooks into play via the wings. Development of this nature is almost invariably bad.

(f) If you intend to attack, be careful to keep a fluid pawn formation: do not block the position or allow your opponent to do so.

(g) Finally, remember that in chess timidity pays no dividends – play aggressively!

Examples from Play: 1. King's Side Attack

When discussing the question of an attack with pawns on a castled king, it was pointed out that it is often advisable to castle on the opposite side. Here is a good example of this type of game taken from club play.

	White	Black
1.	e4	e6
2.	d4	d5
3.	exd5	exd5
4.	Bd3	Nf6
5.	Ne2	Be7
6.	Nbc3	c6
7.	Bf4	Bg4
8.	f3	Bh5

9.	Qd2	Nbd7
10.	Ng3	Bg6
11.	Nf5	0-0
12.	Ne2	Re8
13.	g4	

White, having established a strong knight at f5, judges the moment right for attack. Notice these points:

(a) White's pieces are all in play.

(b) Black's queen's bishop is open to attack from the advancing pawns. Black decided not to play Bxf5, as after gxf5 White would have an open file along which the white rooks would threaten the black king.

(c) White's pawn at f3 immobilizes the knight at f6, the square e4 otherwise providing a splendid outpost for this piece.

13. . . .		Nf8
14. 0-0-0		a5

DIAGRAM 69

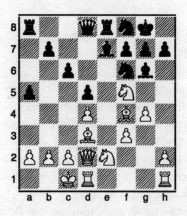

POSITION AFTER BLACK'S 14TH MOVE

Black correctly appraises that the best chance lies in counter-attack on the queen's wing. However, prospects do not look good and the text move is too slow. From now on White dominates the game.

15. h4

White threatens h5, which would force White to take off the knight as the bishop has no escape square.

15. . . .	**h5**
16. Neg3	

White wishes to recapture on f5 with a knight, and so sacrifices a pawn to this end.

16. . . .	**hxg4**
17. fxg4	**Nxg4**

These exchanges are fatal for Black, who now opens the g-file as well as allowing the h-pawn to advance.

18. h5	**Bh7**
19. Qe2	**Nf6**
20. Qg2	

White has gained time and is in a position to exploit the open file. The immediate threat is the curious 21. Nxg7, and the king would not be able to recapture because of 22. Nf5++ Kh8 and 23. Qg7#. The power of the double check is admirably demonstrated: the knight is *en prise* to the bishop and there are notionally three pieces that Black can interpose between the king and the queen. But a double check prescribes a king move and nothing can be done to avert mate.

20. . . .	**Ne6**
21. Be5	

Indirectly attacking the weak g-pawn.

21. . . .	**Kh8**

The black king evades the indirect file attack of the white queen only to walk into the indirect attack of the white bishop on e5. Black could have offered more resistance by playing Ng4, blocking the g-file.

22. h6	**g6**

To avoid the opening of the h-file, which would be terminal, Black is compelled to advance the g-pawn. Now however the knight at f6 is pinned and Black cannot escape the loss of a piece.

23. Nxe7	**Qxe7**
24. Rdf1	**Kg8**
25. Rxf6	**Nf8**
26. Nh5	**Nd7**

Black cannot capture the knight as the pawn is pinned.

27. Bxg6	

An example of bulldozer tactics to crush a weak king's position: Black's last defences are stripped.

27. . . .	**fxg6**
28. Rxg6+	**Bxg6**
29. Qxg6+	**Kf8**
30. Bg7+	**Kg8**
31. h7#	

DIAGRAM 70

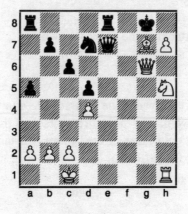

FINAL POSITION

Black watched passively as White's forces gathered strength, instead of initiating early action in the centre or on the queen's side. Black's position was cramped, making it difficult to marshal a defence – notice that at the end of the game, the queen's rook still stood on its starting square.

One lesson at least may be drawn: it rarely pays to adopt wait-and-see tactics in the middle game.

Examples from Play: 2. The Switch Attack

When engaged in a struggle on one wing, an eye should be kept on the possibility of a quick switch-over to the other wing if the opportunity presents itself.

Here is another game in which White never for one moment loses sight of the whole board.

	White	*Black*
1.	e4	e5
2.	Nf3	Nc6
3.	Bb5	a6
4.	Ba4	Nf6
5.	0-0	Nxe4
6.	d4	b5
7.	Bb3	d5
8.	dxe5	Be6

Up to here, identical with the game given in Opening 5 in the last chapter.

	White	Black
9.	Qe2	Be7
10.	Rd1	Na5
11.	Nbd2	Nxd2
12.	Bxd2	Nc4
13.	Bxc4	bxc4
14.	b3	cxb3
15.	axb3	

White has gained a positional advantage. The black a-pawn is isolated on a file open to the white rooks. The threat is Rxa6.

15. . . .	Qc8
16. Ra5	

This square is momentarily safe from bishop attack so White takes the opportunity of doubling rooks.

16. . . .	Qb7
17. Rda1	Bc8
18. Bg5	

DIAGRAM 71

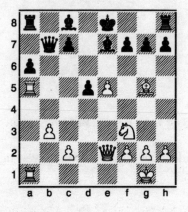

POSITION AFTER WHITE'S 18TH MOVE

An attempt to prevent Black castling. If Black plays now 18. . . . f6, White wins quickly by 19. exf6 and the black bishop is pinned.

18. ...	Bb4
19. R5a4	0-0
20. Qd3	Bd7

A trap. If now 21. Rxa6 Bb5! would win the white queen in exchange for rook, minor piece and pawn. However, Black did not expect White to walk the plank, and his real intention was to establish the bishop at b5, relieving the weak a-pawn and freeing the queen's rook for action elsewhere. Black is blind to White's plan, although White's last move, coupled with the presence of the two white minor pieces on the king's side were a warning that White might not be wholly concerned with what was happening on the queen's side. The next move comes as a complete shock.

21. c3   **Bxa4**

Black can do no better than accept the offer of the exchange.

22. Rxa4   **Bc5**
23. Rh4

Switching to the king's side. White threatens mate on the move by Qxh7.

23. . . .   **f5**

The alternatives were: (a) 23. . . . g6, permitting Bf6 and a set-up similar to example H of Mating Combinations (Chapter 4), when White can force mate in a few moves; or (b) 23. . . . h6, allowing the sacrificial combination 24. Bxh6! and Black's king's position is hopeless. This second type of position – when the king is denuded of pawn protection – has also been referred to previously, an endorsement of how frequently these standard positions can arise.

24. exf6 e.p.

White takes the pawn *en passant*. It cannot be recaptured without quick loss, as Qxh7+ is still threatened.

24. . . .   **g6**
25. Ne5   **c6**
26. Nxg6

As in the previous game, White sacrifices a piece on g6 to break open the position. Here it cannot be taken without mate in two following (26. . . . hxg6   27. Qxg6+ Qg7 28. Qxg7#).

26. . . .	**Rf7**
27. Ne5	**Re8**
28. Qg3	

28. Nxf7 would be a bad mistake. 28. . . . Re1+ 29. Qf1 (forced) Rxf1+ 30. Kxf1 Qxf7 and wins. This bears out the maxim "Watch the back rank."

28. . . .	**Qa7**

Black cannot well avoid the double check, for Kf8 or Kh8 would be met with decisive checks from the bishop and knight respectively.

29. Bh6+	**Kh8**
30. Ng6+	**Kg8**

DIAGRAM 72

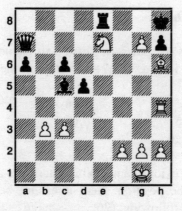

FINAL POSITION

Black cannot capture the knight: 30. . . . hxg6 31. Bf7++ Kg8 32. Rh8#.

31. Ne7++	Kh8
32. Qg7+	Rxg7
33. fxg7#	

A delightfully conducted attack. (See diagram 72.)

Examples from Play: 3. The Centre Breakthrough

A breakthrough in the centre in the early stages of the game is not common, since it can only be achieved when the opposition is disproportionately weak. This example shows condign punishment meted out to a timid player.

	White	*Black*
1.	c4	e5
2.	Nf3	e4
3.	Nd4	d5
4.	e3	c5
5.	Nb3	d4
6.	d3	

White was worried about being left with a backward d-pawn.

6.	...	exd3
7.	Qxd3	Nc6
8.	exd4	cxd4

Black has got a passed pawn in the centre. Can it be held? If so, White's game is already bad as the pawn exercises restraint over the white minor pieces. White will take at least two moves to bring another piece to bear on the intruder (Nbd2–f3), and meanwhile the queen is exposed to attack.

9. a3

White is afraid of Nb4 because after 10. Qe4+ Be6 11. Nxd5 Qxd5 12. Qxd5 Nc2+ 13. K moves, Nxd5 and Black has won a piece for a pawn. This line is by no means forced however, and the text is a waste of time.

9. ...	Qf6
10. N1d2	Bf5
11. Ne4	

This loses, but White had nothing better due to Black's command of the centre.

11. ...	Qe6

Pinning the knight and threatening to win it next move. Observe how the white pieces get tied up in trying to prevent the loss of this piece.

12. f3	Nf6
13. Nd2	

Since the knight on e4 is unable to move, this means the knight on f3.

13. ...	0-0-0

White is completely tied up. The text brings the rook to guard the advanced pawn. White can do nothing about the terrible threat of 14. . . Ne5! attacking the queen and preparing a further advance of the formidable and now secure pawn.

14. Kd1

To unpin the knight.

14. ...	**Ne5**
15. Qb3	**d3**
16. Nxf6	**gxf6**
17. Qa4	

Paralysis has set in, and White is reduced to moving the queen again.

17. ...   Bc5

Black guards the a-pawn, brings the last minor piece into play and unites the rooks, all in the one move.

18. Nb3   Nxf3

DIAGRAM 73

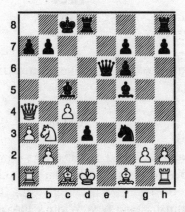

POSITION AFTER BLACK'S 18TH MOVE

An unnecessary sacrifice. Black could have won more convincingly by playing d2, followed, when White takes the pawn, by Be3, leaving White hopelessly pinned.

19. gxf3

White has no option but to accept: Qe1# was threatened. Here 19. Bd2 was useless 19. . . . Nxd2 20. Nxd2 Bg4+ 21. Nf3 (not 21. Kc1 Qe1#) Rhe8 22. Kc1 (22. Qa5 is no better) Bxf3 23. gxf3 Qe1+ 24. Qd1 Be3+ etc.

19. . . .	d2

The pawn which has been the cause of all White's troubles is now sacrificed to force the win. Whichever white piece captures (although again there is no option) will be pinned.

20. Bxd2	Rhe8
21. Bh3	

White had to prevent mate at e1.

21. . . .	Qe2+
22. Kc1	Bxh3
23. Re1	Qxe1+!

A mistake, overlooking Black's queen sacrifice. The best defence was Nxc5.

23. . . .	Qxe1+!
24. Bxe1	Rxe1+
25. Kc2	Bf5+
26. Kc3	Re3#

A pleasing finish. Note how White's forces were split in two by the centre thrust and how, until near the end, neither of the white bishops or rooks had even moved. In the final position it will be seen that both the centre files are controlled by the black rooks and both bishops are occupying the best possible squares relative to the position, whereas not one of the white pieces is well placed.

Examples from Play: 4. The Queen's Side Attack

The Q-side attack differs fundamentally from the K-side attack in that there is no obvious target. This is only true in the broad sense, for in effect any weakness constitutes a target; but a weakness is not strictly a weakness unless it can be exploited. A Q-side attack may be desirable for one or more of several reasons; it may be to counter a K-side attack, it may be because the K-side is either blockaded or barren of opportunity, or it may be because the dispersal of the pieces is such as to be conducive to action on this wing. In the Q-side attack the balance of pawns engaged is of prime importance. By early exchanges it is common to find one player left with three pawns against two on the Q-side and with, say, three against four in the centre and on the K-side. In any case, the attacker's plan should be governed to a large extent by the pawn ratio and the pawn structure, for weaknesses are created primarily by pawns through their inability to retrace their steps.

The attacker therefore launches an assault with the intention of exploiting (or creating) a weakness in order to achieve an advantage in material, space or time.

The attacker must be prepared to change his plan at any apparent change of weaknesses (i.e. when the defender disposes of one weakness only to create another).

The example appended is from Master play (Euwe-Medina London 1946), and I have selected it for its simplicity of idea and execution.

	White	Black
1.	d4	d5

2. c4	e6
3. Nc3	Nf6
4. Bg5	Be7
5. e3	h6
6. Bh4	0-0
7. Rc1	Ne4
8. Bxe7	Qxe7
9. cxd5	Nxc3

Not of course 9. . . . exd5 10. Nxd5!

10. Rxc3	exd5
11. Bd3	c6
12. Ne2	Nd7
13. 0-0	Nf6
14. Qb1	

Up to here the game has followed well-trodden paths. White now perceives that the king's side is sterile of opportunity, the centre is closed (there is little chance of being able to force e4), and therefore the future of the game lies on the queen's wing.

Although White has the pawn minority on this side (two to three), the Black pieces are not well placed whilst White can manoeuvre freely. The text move prepares the advance of the b-pawn.

14. . . .	a5

Temporarily delaying the advance of the pawn.

15. a3	Bd7

White has succeeded in creating a small weakness in the black position: either the b- or c-pawn is going to be permanently backward.

| 16. b4 | axb4 |
| 17. axb4 | Ra4 |

Black has obtained compensation in the open rook's file. There follows a typical manoeuvre in which Black moves the rook up to attack an undefended piece and is thereby able to double rooks on the file.

18. Rb3

Not 18. b5 cxb5 19. Bxb5 Rb4 20. Rb3 Bxb5 21. Rxb4 Bxe2 22. Rxb7 Qe4 forcing the exchange of queens and leaving Black with a material advantage. Subtle resources frequently lurk in innocent-looking positions.

18. ...	Rfa8
19. b5	g6
20. bxc6	Bxc6

Now the black b-pawn is isolated. The d-pawn is also isolated. Black could have avoided both these contingencies by recapturing with the pawn, but then the bishop would have been shut in, a white rook would have been able to occupy the seventh rank, and the advance c5 would probably never have been playable.

21. Bb5	Ra2
22. Nc3	R2a3
23. Rc1	Ng4
24. Rxa3	Rxa3
25. Nd1	

Black threatened Qh4 with a winning attack by: 25. . . . Nxe3 26. fxe3 Qxe3+ 27. Kh1 Rxc3.

| 25. ... | Qc7 |

26. g3

Black threatened Qxh2+. White correctly estimates Black's attack to be of little consequence as Black has not now time to take advantage of White's weakened pawn position.

26. . . .	**Qa5**
27. Bxc6	**bxc6**
28. h3	**Nf6**
29. Rxc6	

The weak pawn falls. Black's next move enables White to switch flanks and proceed to a direct attack on the black king.

29. . . .	**Ra1**
30. Qb8+	**Kg7**
31. Qe5	

Wrong would have been 31. Rxf6, hoping for 31. . . . Kxf6 32. Qe5# because of the reply 31. . . . Rxd1+ 32. Kg2 Qe1 and now White, faced with a mate threat, has nothing better than 33. Rxf7+ Kxf7 34. Qc7+ Kf6 35. Qd6+ etc.

31. . . .	**Rxd1+**

White has not sacrificed a piece because the black knight is pinned and cannot be saved.

32. Kh2	**Qd8**

If 32. . . . Qe1, White gets there first with 33. Qxf6+ and mate in two.

33. Rd6	**Qxd6**

There is nothing better. If 33. . . . Qc7 34. Qxf6+ Kh7

DIAGRAM 74

POSITION AFTER WHITE'S 31ST MOVE

35. Rd8 threatens mate on the move and the queen must be given up. Or 33. ... . Qe8 34. Qxf6+ Kh7 35. Kh2 and the black d-pawn will fall. But not 35. Rd8? Qe4+ and Black wins.

34. Qxd6   Rd2
35. Qe5

And Black prolonged the game a few more moves before resigning.

The game, logical throughout, is a lesson in model play on the part of White who created weaknesses and exploited them sufficiently to win a pawn, and then attacked the compromised defence structure that remained. Even if Black had not gone in for the faulty combination that cost the game, it would not have been long before White's extra pawn would have made itself felt. The isolated d-pawn would also have been difficult to defend against the combined assault of the White pieces, and the bolder but swifter death was to be preferred.

Combinations

To give you practice in assessing positions where it is often possible to force immediate wins, some examples from play are given. In all cases White, to move, wins. No solution is longer than six moves, and the examples are given in order of difficulty. Solutions are given on page 158.

DIAGRAM 75

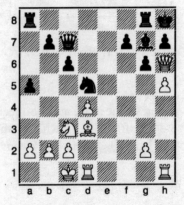

DIAGRAM 76

DIAGRAM 77

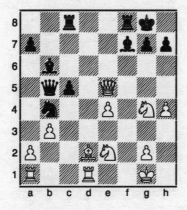

DIAGRAM 78

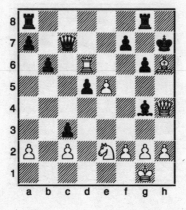

DIAGRAM 79

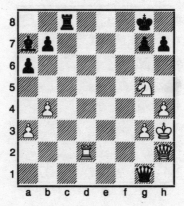

DIAGRAM 80

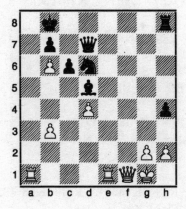

Solutions

Diagram 75: 1. Qxh7+ Kxh7 2. hxg6#.

Diagram 76: 1. Qxh7+ Kxh7 2. Nxf6+ Kh8 3. Ng6#.

Diagram 77: 1. Qxg7+ Kxg7 2. Bc3+ Kg6 (Kg8 3. Nh6#)
3. Nf4#.

Diagram 78: 1. Bf8 dis+ Bh5 2. Qxh5+ gxh5 3. Rh6#.

Diagram 79: 1. Rd8+ Rxd8 2. Qa2+ (and now White has the
Philidor's Legacy) Kh8   3. Nf7+ Kg8   4. Nh6+ Kh8
5. Qg8+ Rxg8 6. Nf7#.

Diagram 80: 1. Ra8+ Kxa8 2. Ra1+ Kb8 3. Ra8+ Kxa8
4. Qa1+ Kb8 5. Qa7+ Kc8 6. Qa8#.

7

THE END GAME

Introduction

Very few players get excited about the end game; it is the calm after the storm, the anti-climax. This is probably why the average player manages it so badly; it is certain that more won games are dissipated in the ending than in the opening and middle game combined.

There is a tendency to speed up the play when there are only a few pieces left on the board – and the "obvious" line of play is often the wrong one. The subtleties that exist in this branch of the game are prodigious, and seemingly hopeless positions may be redeemed by witch-like manoeuvres. There is an old chess adage that runs, "If you see a good move, look for a better one", and nowhere does it hold more true than in the end game.

The first prejudice that must be destroyed is that the end game is stereotyped and uninteresting. It demands imagination, patience and accurate calculation. A study of the various endings also accords a valuable insight into the powers, both latent and active, of the individual chess pieces.

The Opposition

In order to begin to understand the theory governing the end game, a clear conception of the "opposition" and what it implies is essential.

If two kings are facing each other on the same file or rank with one vacant square only between them, the player who DOES NOT HAVE the move is said to have the "opposition". A corollary is the diagonal opposition – two kings standing on the same diagonal with one vacant square between them. Again the player who DOES NOT HAVE the move has the opposition.

The opposition is only considered to be in effect if the player who is not possessed of it has no other piece except the king that can be moved without incurring disadvantage.

To have the opposition is almost always desirable, and is often a winning advantage for it permits the king to gain territory at the expense of the enemy king, and perhaps eventually to penetrate the enemy pawn position.

Look at diagram 81. Here the kings are facing each other and the pawn formations are static and to all intents symmetrical. If Black is to move, White wins. If White is to move, the game is a draw.

(a) Black to move. 1. . . . Ke6 2. Kc5 (the white king is at once able to attack Black's pawns) Ke5 3. Kxb5 Kd4 (only now is the black king able to pass to attack the white pawns) 4. Kxa4 Ke3 5. b5 Kxf3 6. b6 Kxg4 7. b7 f3 8. b8Q and wins. However, the conclusion requires some care: 8. . . . f2 9. Qb5 Kf4 (9. . . . Kf3? 10. Qxg5 f1Q 11. Qf5+ Ke2 12. Qxf1+ Kxf1 13. Kb5 and the a-pawn queens) 10. Qe2 Kg3 11. Kb4 Kg2 (there is nothing better) 12. Qg4+ Kh1 13. Qh5+ Kg1 14. Qxg5+ and again White can give up the queen for the f-pawn, marching the a-pawn through to promotion. (There are other ways of winning this ending.)

Supposing if, instead of 1. . . . Ke6, Black had played 1. . . . Kc6. Now White's task is easier: 2. Ke5 Kc7 (the diagonal opposition, but now tactical considerations take precedence); 3. Kf5 Kd6 4. Kxg5 Ke5 5. Kh6 and White promotes the g-pawn quickly. Note that the white king *in advance* and to *one side* of the passed pawn assures its promotion. Black can do nothing; viz: 5. . . . Kf6 6. g5+ Kf7 7. Kh7 (preventing the black

DIAGRAM 81

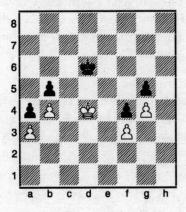

king occup ing the promotion square) Kf8 8. g6 Ke7 9. g7 Kf7 10. g8Q+.

(b) White to move. 1. Ke4 Ke6 2. Kd4 Kd6 and the white king cannot pass, and draw by repetition of moves will follow (see Chapter 1).

Now remove the four pawns on the king's side and study the position again. What result with each player to move? Answer – as before: White to move draws; Black to move, White wins.

(a) Black to move. 1. . . . Kc6 (Black has lost the opposition) 2. Ke5 (White elects to penetrate the fifth rank instead: to have taken the opposition would merely have maintained the status quo) Kc7 3. Kd5 Kb6 (now the importance of White's Ke5 is evident: Black is obliged again to surrender the opposition in order to protect the undefended b-pawn) 4. Kd6! (White, having gained territory, now takes the opposition) Kb7 5. Kc5 Ka6 6. Kc6 (the opposition again:

Black is compelled to relinquish the pawn) Ka7 8. Kxb5 Kb7
9. Kxa4 and White will have no difficulty in winning.

(b) White to move. 1. Ke4 Ke6 2. Kd4 Kd6 and we have
the same crab-like repetition of moves as before, with neither
party yielding ground.

Now replace the four pawns on the king's side and remove
the four pawns on the queen's side. Is the result materially
affected? The answer is yes – White can only draw with or
without the move.

(a) Black to move. 1. . . . Kc6! 2. Ke5 Kc5 3. Kf5 Kd4
4. Kxg5 Ke3 5. Kh5 Kxf3 6. g5 Ke2 7. g6 f3 8. g7 f2
9. g8Q f1Q and since both sides have a king and queen left,
the game will be drawn (there are sometimes exceptions to
this rule). But if instead 1. . . . Ke6 Black would lose after 2.
Ke4 Kf6 3. Kd5 (temporarily surrendering the opposition, but
penetrating the same rank as the undefended black pawn) Kf7
4. Ke5 (threatening to win the pawn in two moves) Kg6
5. Ke6 Kg7 6. Kf5 Kh6 7. Kf6 Kh7 8. Kxg5 Kg7 9. Kxf4
and wins.

(b) White to move. 1. Ke4 and Black takes up the opposition again by 1. . . . Ke6, forcing a repetition of moves. If
Black opts instead to advance among the white pawns, the
game still ends in a draw: 1. . . . Kc5 2. Kf5 Kd4 and draws
as in (a) above.

The thoughtful reader might ask: Why, in a symmetrical
position, does White manage to draw with the move whereas
Black loses? Study diagram 81 again. It will be seen that the
position is not in fact symmetrical; the white king has the
advantage of position. If both kings were moved one rank
down the board (to stand on d3 and d5 respectively), the game
would be drawn whoever had the move.

King and Pawn v King

In this ending, the theme is only carried a stage further. Turn back to diagram 11, page 42. In example (a) White to move wins by Kc6 or Ka6. Because of the pawn at b7, the black king is not able to ʿake up the opposition and must immediately yield ground. This ending (K + P v K) is simply a fight for the opposition with the odds on the superior force. If a pawn is mobile (not far advanced) it can be used to gain the opposition by interpolating a move.

There are some rules that can be used to guide the player:

(a) With an a- or h-pawn, the game is always drawn if the lone king can reach the promotion square or if able to confine the opponent's king on the file in front of the pawn.

(b) If the pawn is advancing level with or in front of the supporting king, the lone king always draws with the opposition.

(c) A king two squares in front of its pawn will always win since a pawn move will ensure the opposition.

(d) A king one square in front of its pawn will win if in possession of the opposition, or if the pawn is on the fifth rank.

King and Pawn v King and Pawn

The various cases of K and P v K and P are most important as they are forever recurring. We are not concerned with instances where one pawn immediately falls, or marches through to queen several moves before its rival; but those in which the result may be obscure.

(a) If two pawns stand facing each other away from the edge of the board, and both kings are able to approach the opposing pawns, then the side which approaches first will lose if such approach is not from behind.
WHITE: K on f5, P on d4. BLACK: K on b5, P on d5.
1. Ke5? Kc4 2. Ke6 (White is compelled to leave the pawn)

Kxd4 and wins. If White approaches from behind, however, the result will be a draw: 1. Ke6 Kc6 (not 1. . . . Kc4? 2. Ke5 and it is Black who must give up the pawn); 2. Ke5 Kc7 3. Kxd5 Kd7 and Black has got the opposition.

(b) Where each side has a pawn marching to queen, and the promotions are consecutive, the result is usually a draw, but not always. Here is an exception: WHITE: K on d2, P on h5. BLACK: K on d4, P on a3. 1. h6 a2 2. h7 a1Q 3. h8Q+ K moves 4. Qxa1 and wins.

This possibility prompts the necessity for attention to all pre-promotion king moves. WHITE: K on g7, Ps on b2, h6. BLACK: K on c2, Ps on b3, h7. 1. Kxh7 Kxb2 2. Kg8 Kc3? (this move loses: any other move except Ka1 or Kb1 draws) 3. h7 b2 4. h8Q+. Now we see the importance of careful king-play. The black king is in check and will not be able to queen the pawn. 4. . . . Kc2 5. Qh7+ (the ending is instructive and is therefore given in full; White must play to drive the black king in front of the pawn by a series of checks, permitting the white king to approach) Kc1 6. Qc7+ Kd1 7. Qd6+ Kc1 8. Qc5+ Kd1 9. Qd4+ Kc1 10. Qc3+ Kb1 (now the white king can approach) 11. Kf7 Ka2 12. Qc2 (pinning the pawn) Ka1 (not 12. . . . Ka3 13. Qb1) 13. Qa4+ Kb1 14. Ke6 Kc1 15. Qc4+ Kd1 16. Qb3+ Kc1 17. Qc3+ Kb1 18. Kd5 Ka2 19. Qc2 (the same cycle) Ka1 20. Qa4+ Kb1 21. Kd4 Kc1 22. Qc4+ Kd1 23. Qd3+ Kc1 24. Kc3 b1Q 25. Qd2#. If 24. . . . b1N+, Black has insufficient force to draw.

(c) In the foregoing example, Black was left with a king and a knight's pawn against king and queen and was unable to save the game. If instead the pawn had been on a bishop's or rook's file, the result would have been a draw, due to a stale-mate threat.

(i) **Bishop's Pawn.** WHITE: K on g7, P on h7. BLACK: K on d2, P on c3. 1. h8Q c2 2. Qd8+ Kc3 3. Qc7+ Kb2 4. Qb6+ Ka1 5. Qa5+ Kb1 (Black always threatens to promote the pawn, giving the white king no time to approach) 6. Qb4+ Ka1 7. Qa3+ Kb1 8. Qb3+ Ka1! (instead of moving in front of the pawn, which the king was forced to do in the previous example, the black king moves into the corner for now if White plays 9. Qxc2, Black is stalemated) 9. Qc3+ Kb1 10. Qb3+ Ka1 and White can make no headway.

(ii) **Rook's Pawn.** WHITE: K on g7, P on h7. BLACK: K on c2, P on a3. 1. h8Q a2 2. Qh2+ Kb1 3. Qg1+ Kb2 4. Qf2+ Kb1 5. Qe1+ Kb2 (not 5. . . . Kc2 6. Qa1) 6. Qb4+ Kc1 7. Qa3+ Kb1 8. Qb3+ Ka1 when Black has no move. To avoid stalemate, White must move the queen away so the white king will never have time to approach.

A lesson to be learned from the above examples is the method of bringing the queen up the board by a series of checks, which can be done vertically, as in (i), or horizontally, as in (ii).

These are the only three cases of K and P v K and P endings that are likely to cause you any difficulty. There are certain exceptions, but being rare in practical play they are not worth our investigation here. To recapitulate: in the cases where one side queens first, and the other side then advances a pawn to the seventh rank supported by the king on the seventh or eighth ranks (also the sixth rank in the majority of cases), the game is a draw if the pawn is on the bishop's or rook's file, a win for the stronger force if on any other file – always provided, of course, that the other king cannot immediately influence the play. If the second player can only advance the pawn to the sixth rank on the move following promotion, the game is always won by the first player regardless of the position of the kings.

King and Two Pawns v King and One
This is nearly always a win for the superior force, but there are, nevertheless, numerous positions in which the game is drawn. The two most common cases are:

(i) The two pawns are on opposite wings with the single pawn facing one of them. Suppose White is the superior force in this case. Then White wins by deserting the solitary wing pawn, moving across to the other side of the board, capturing the black piece and queening the remaining pawn; for Black must attend to the unwatched pawn, which will march to queen if not intercepted and captured. Only in unusual cases can the weaker force draw in an ending of this nature.

(ii) The three pawns and two kings are more or less together. It is then simply a question again of the stronger party deserting one of the pawns at the right moment and going for the other, or of exchanging a pawn in order to get a won position in the K and P v K category.

Diagram 82 illustrates four positions not uncommon in this type of ending.

(a) Black draws with or without the move. Black has only to keep the king close to the single pawn. If White advances the b-pawn, the resulting exchange will leave White with the a-pawn which, as we know, is insufficient to win.

DIAGRAM 82

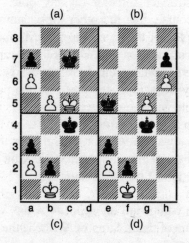

(b) White wins with an immediate sacrifice regardless of the white king position. 1. g6 hxg6 2. h7 and queens next move. Or 1. . . . Kf6 2. gxh7 and the pawn on h6 prevents the black king approaching.

(c) Drawn, regardless of who has the move. White alternates the king between b1 and c2 and any attempt by Black to interfere will result in stalemate.

(d) This position is like (c) but away from the edge of the board. In this and similar positions, the stronger force wins, with or without the move. 1. Kg2 Kf4 2. Kf1 Ke4 3. Kg2 Kd4 4. Kf1 Kc3 5. Kg2 Kd2 6. Kf1 Kd1 7. Kg2 Kxe2 and wins.

King and Two Pawns v King and Two Pawns
This ending, and endings involving more than two pawns a side, are but extensions of those we have already examined. The opposition remains paramount.

A well-known stratagem, not often seen in actual play, is the establishment of a passed pawn when both sides have three pawns, line abreast, facing each other. WHITE: K on h1, Ps on a5, b5, c5. BLACK: K on h3, Ps on a7, b7, c7. Although the black king can reach the pawns first, White wins by: 1. b6 cxb6 2. a6 bxa6 3. c6 If 1. . . . axb6 the procedure is the same; viz: 2. c6 etc.

King, Minor Piece, Pawn v King and Minor Piece
The issue at stake here is a simple one: can the pawn be queened? The important point to remember is that the weaker force has only to sacrifice the piece for the pawn to draw. A simple example will show how important it is for the stronger player to keep the pawn mobile in order to retain any winning chances.

WHITE: K on h1, N on b1. BLACK: K on g3, N on g5, P on e5. 1. Nd2 Kh3? 2. Nf3 and now 2. . . . Nxf3 gives stalemate, and any other move allows White to capture the pawn leaving Black with insufficient force.

Bishops of opposite colours invariably draw in this type of

ending, but with bishops of the same colour the stronger side can often force a victory, the method being to drive the opposing bishop from the vital diagonal by offering an exchange at the moment when such an exchange would yield the opposition. If the opposing king is in front of the pawn, however, and cannot be driven away by checks from the bishop, the game is always drawn.

The N and P v B and the B and P v N are the two most interesting – and most common – endings in this category.

In the first case the superior force endeavours to block the bishop diagonal by intervening the knight, and in the second case to force the win by placing the bishop so as to prohibit the knight from approaching the pawn. The power of the bishop over the knight, which is complementary to the knight's power over the bishop, can be seen if a white bishop is placed on e4 and a black knight on h4. Here the knight is unable to move without being captured, although the bishop, in turn, may not move to any of the squares in the knight's field without being exposed to the same risk. This setting is normally unfavourable to the knight, but under certain conditions it may be advantageous, particularly if the bishop is nearer the edge of the board than the knight.

If there are more pawns on the board, the matter becomes purely an elaboration of the same theme. The reader is advised to turn back to Chapter 2 for general hints on handling the minor pieces in the ending.

King and Minor Piece v King and Pawns

With two pawns, this ending is resolved to a case of where the player with the piece will sacrifice it for one pawn in order to be left with the opposition in the ensuing play, thereby assuring the draw.

If the pawns are on opposite sides of the board, or at least separated, the outcome is not difficult to foresee. Two disunited pawns can frequently "squeeze" a bishop: WHITE:

K on h2, Ps on b5, g6. BLACK: K on h4, B on e2. White wins by 1. b6 Bf3 2. g7 Bd5 and now the advance of either pawn will force the bishop to capture, allowing the other to promote. With a knight instead of the bishop, the two-pawn "squeeze" is even easier. These cases are, of course, assuming that the kings cannot affect the play.

If a minor piece is opposed by three pawns, it is usually possible to promote one of the latter with correct play, but there are a number of positions where this ending is only a draw.

Queen and Pawn Endings

In this type of ending, the position of the kings is of the utmost importance. If a king is exposed to a series of checks from which there is no sanctuary, the pawn ratio will have no bearing on the game, which will result in a draw.

If, however, the king is able to reach a position of security, a mobile extra pawn will be sufficient to win, it being escorted to promotion by the queen.

Rook and Pawn Endings

These are by far the most important, as they are the most common form of ending, due, in part, to the normally delayed development of the rooks in the opening and middle game which enhances their chances of survival.

As has been remarked elsewhere, when both sides have two rooks left, the drawing opportunities that present themselves to the side possessed of the inferior pawn position, structurally or numerically, are greater, on average, than occur when each side has only one rook remaining on the board.

The endings involving single rooks and pawns are much the more usual however, and the strategy they embrace may be applied in measure to the positions involving the weightier force.

The main features of this type of ending may be conveniently tabulated.

(a) **Stopping Promotion.** A rook can prevent the promotion of a pawn assisted by a rook by moving onto the same file as the pawn either behind or in front of it. Place a white rook on b8, a black rook on h2 and a black pawn on b2. The black pawn cannot move without being captured, and the black rook is unable to leave the second rank. Note that the white rook can move up and down the file without in any way relaxing vigil on the advanced pawn. Now leave the two black pieces where they are and place the white rook on b1. Again the black rook cannot leave the rank, but now Black can play Rc2, and the white rook is unable to move along the rank on account of Rc1 followed by b1. From this we see that the rook is best employed *behind* an enemy pawn. In these two examples the black rook is badly placed. Now consider the following position: white rook on b1, black rook on b8 and black pawn on b2. Here it is Black who retains mobility – the white rook is unable to move without allowing the promotion of the pawn. If the white king is able to reach the pawn first, it will fall; if the black king reaches it first the white rook will be lost or the pawn will be successfully promoted – the unhappy choice resting with White. If, in the example just given, the two rooks are interchanged, White's position is immeasurably improved for similar reasons.

(b) **The Promotion Check.** This may arise out of the last example, and should be carefully watched. WHITE: K on g2, R on b8. BLACK: K on g7, R on b1, P on b2. The white king can only shuffle between g2 and h2. Any move to the third rank loses at once: 1. Kg3 Rg1+ and promotes next move. More subtle is the pitfall 1. Kf2? Rh1! and if 2. Rxb2 Rh2+ (the skewer) and the rook is lost.

(c) **Rook and Pawn v Rook.** The convenient rule for this ending is that if the king of the weaker force can reach the promotion square of the pawn, the game is drawn; if it can be prevented from reaching it, the game is won by the stronger force. An exception, as always, is the rook's pawn, which in certain positions is only a draw. There is considerable finesse necessary to achieve the promotion, even after the opposing king has been shut off, as the perpetual check remains recourse for the weaker player which may not be easily discounted.

(d) **Rook v Pawn(s).** Two important points to be remembered here. Firstly, that two united pawns that are able to reach the sixth rank without capture will win against a rook, provided that the opposing king cannot interfere; and secondly, that a king and single pawn advanced to the fourth rank or beyond will draw against a rook, provided that the other king is unable to interfere. The first case can be easily proven by just setting the pawns up, placing the rook anywhere on the board where it is unable to capture either of the pawns immediately, and then attempting to arrest promotion. One pawn will certainly fall, but the other will reach the eighth rank safely, and the balance (queen v rook) is then sufficient to achieve victory.

The second rule is as easy to verify as the first, but why the stipulation "advanced to the fourth rank"? Because, if only on the third rank, the king can be cut off by the rook, the pawn permitted to advance and then attacked and captured before the king can reach it.

Here is an example to clarify the method: WHITE: K on h8, R on a1. BLACK: K on g6, P on h5. With Black to move, the fourth rank is attained by Kg5 and the game is drawn. But White, to play, wins by 1. Ra5 h4 2. Kg8 h3 (if the pawn is not advanced, the white king will return to decide the issue) 3. Kf8 h2 4. Ra1 Kg5 5. Rh1 Kg4 6. Rxh2 and wins. It will be seen that if the black king had been one square nearer he would have been defending the pawn, and the result would have been a draw.

This "cutting off" of the king is an important feature of rook and pawn end games. An enemy rook ensconced on the seventh (i.e. on the second) rank can be very disturbing if one's king has not left the back rank.

Conclusion

So far we have covered, if very superficially, the entire field
of end game play. Many of the points stressed require elaboration and, in certain cases, qualification, but essentially the
fundamentals are there. Few average players know more
about this phase of the game than these fundamentals, and
many are not even conversant with all of them. Three
endings from play are now given which demonstrate that
charm and subtlety may be concealed in apparently dull
positions.

Examples from Play: 1. Pawn Ending

The position in diagram 83, with Black to play, was reached
in a match game between two strong amateurs. Pawns are
level, and at first glance it appears as though a draw is the
likely result. A closer examination will disclose that there is
considerably more play in the position than at first meets the
eye.

DIAGRAM 83

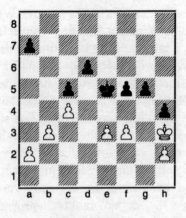

BLACK TO PLAY

White	Black
1. ...	f4
2. e4	

This is forced. If 2. exf4+ Kxf4 3. Kg2 Ke3 and Black will win the f-pawn, and with it the game. To give up the pawn is equally suicidal: 2. Kg2 fxe3 3. Kf1 Kd4 4. Ke2 h3 5. a3 Kc3 6. Kxe3 Kxb3 winning easily.

Black now observes that White has an uncompromised pawn majority in that theatre of the board bounded by the a- and e-files. Every uncompromised pawn majority (i.e. where no pawn is doubled) must yield a passed pawn so any incursion by the black king could prove fatal. For example: 2. ... Kd4 3. Kg4 Ke3 4. b4! Kd4 (or 4. ... cxb4 5. c5 dxc5 6. e5 and queens in three moves) 5. bxc5 Kxc5 (5. ... dxc5 would allow 6. Kf5, when the pawn would march to queen) 6. Kxg5 Kxc4 7. K x either pawn, winning.

2. ...	Kf6
3. Kg4	Kg6
4. h3	a5
5. a4	

These pawn moves are important and are often decisive in pawn endings. White has the opposition, and the black king is forced to move, allowing the white king to penetrate. If, in the position now reached, White had the move instead of Black, White would have lost, being compelled to advance a pawn: 1. e5 dxe5 2. b4 cxb4 3. c5 b3 4. c6 b2 5. c7 b1Q 6. c8Q Qg1#.

If instead of 4. ... a5 Black had played 4. ... a6, White's reply would have been 5. a3 and not 5. a4? a5 and Black has the opposition.

5. ...	Kh6

Not of course 5. . . . Kf6 6. Kh5 followed by Kxg5 winning for White.

6. Kf5

And now it looks as though White is going to force the win.

6. . . .   Kh5

White must select from several moves here. The interesting pawn sacrifice: 7. b4 is not quite sound. 7. . . . cxb4 (if axb4 White wins by 8. a5 b3 9. a6 b2 10. a7 b1Q 11. a8Q Qb2 (the only move to stop the threatened mate at h8) 12. Qe8+ Kh6 13. Qg6#) 8. c5 dxc5 9. e5 b3 10. e6 b2 11. e7 b1Q+ winning.

The obvious 7. Ke6 is fatal, as White would succumb to a trap: 7. . . . g4! (Black's uncompromised pawn majority on the king's side is set into motion to yield a passed pawn now that the hostile king is out of range) 8. fxg4+ (there is nothing better) Kg5 and the f-pawn goes through to queen.

White is therefore left with the alternatives of playing Kf6 or e5. If the king advances, the game will be drawn, for Black would have nothing better than to return with the king (Kh6) which will result in a repetition of moves. Black could not now play 7. . . . g4 as White could respond 8. hxg4+ Kh6 9. g5+ Kh5 10. g6 h3 11. g7 h2 12. g8Q h1Q 13. Q mates.

Supposing White plays 7. e5, what happens then? Black must capture: 7. . . . dxe5 and White can do no better than recapture: 8. Kxe5. Now 8. . . . g4 loses for Black. 9. fxg4+ Kg5 10. Ke4, and Black must yield the pawn. After White's eighth move, both sides have a clear majority on one side of the board, and neither can afford to take the initiative in establishing a passed pawn without conceding the game to the other. One illustration will serve to demonstrate this: 8. . . . Kg6 9. b4? cxb4 10. Kd4 Kf6 11. c5 Ke6 12. Kc4 Kd7 13. Kd4 and now g4 14. fxg4 f3 15. Ke3 b3 wins.

In consequence of these continuations, the game was abandoned as a draw. A highly instructive end game.

Examples from Play: 2. Bishop and Pawns

This example is also from amateur play. Although pawns are level, the bishops are of the same colour – a factor which is important, as we have commented that, in endings of this nature, the side possessing even the slightest advantage in position is often able to force the win.

Here the black king is confined to the edge of the board, and White, with considerable ingenuity, is able to exploit this weakness to secure the win.

	White	*Black*
1.	...	**g3**

Black has a choice of five plausible moves here, all of which lose. The text appears to be the most promising, for White is unable to play 2. hxg3 on account of 2. . . . h2!

DIAGRAM 84

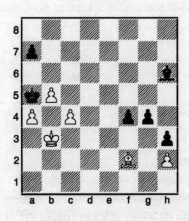

BLACK TO PLAY

2. Bxa7		**Bf8**

Black cannot play 2. . . . gxh2 as after 3. c5 the mate 4. Bb6 would be unstoppable.

3. Bb8

Threatening 4. Bc7#.

3. . . .		**Bc5**

On 3. . . . Kb6 White would have continued 4. a5+ Kc5 (Kb7 also loses) 5. Bxf4 and wins, as after 5. . . . gxh2 6. Bxh2, Black cannot play Bd6 as this would permit 7. Bg1#.

It is amusing to note that after 3. . . . Kb6 White would have to play carefully if he accepted the pawn at once: 4. Bxf4 g2 5. Be3+? (5. a5+ wins) Bc5 6. a5+ Kxa5 7. Bxc5 g1Q 8. Bxg1 stalemate!

4. Bc7+	**Bb6**
5. Bxf4	

Threatening Bd2#, as the black piece now blocks the king's flight square.

5. . . .	**Bc5**
6. Bc7+	**Bb6**

A vicious see-saw. Compare the example given under "The Seventh Rank" in the last chapter, page 135.

7. Bxg3

And now White wins comfortably.

Let us examine the other lines available to Black on the first move:

(A) 1. . . . f3. This loses quickly. 2. c5 (threatening mate by Be1) Bd2 (the only move) 3. Bh4 and Black cannot avert the mate at d8.

(B) 1. . . . a6. Now 2. b6! Bf8 3. c5 (Be1 is again threatened) Bxc5 4. Bxc5 g3 5. b7 gxh2 6. b8 (Q, R or B) and White mates next move.

(C) 1. . . . Bg7. 2. c5 Bc3 3. Bh4 – the mixture as before.

(D) 1. . . . Bf8. 2. c5 Bxc5 (this sacrifice is forced, as the mate at e1 is again threatened) 3. Bxc5 g3 (if 3. . . . . a6, the continuation is 4. b6, as in (B) above) 4. Bd6 (the mating threat is now Bc7) Kb6 5. Bxf4 and White wins easily by forcing home a queen's-side pawn.

Examples from Play: 3. Rook and Pawns

As stated previously, this type of ending is by far the most common, and the position in diagram 85 is as prosaic as one could wish for. In its banality lies its importance, however, for most players, as Black, would be content with a draw. This ending was reached in a game between players of international repute (Najdorf-Szabo Saltsjöbaden Interzonal 1948), and Black, far from being satisfied with a draw, perceived that by exact play a win could be forced. Every move is an object-lesson in timing and precision.

	White	*Black*
1.	Rd7	

Preventing the advance of the black king.

1.	...	Rb3

Cutting off the white king from the defence of the f-pawn.

2.	Ra7	Rd3

Black's task is by no means easy. In general, a pawn plus in

DIAGRAM 85

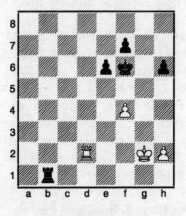

WHITE TO PLAY

rook-and-pawn endings is of little importance if the pawns are all on one side of the board and the kings are in their own territories.

3. Rb7

White plays at "wait and see".

3. ...   Kg7!

A profound move. If 3. . . . Kg6 4. f5+ exf5 (4. . . . Kxf5 5. Rxf7+); and Black, although two pawns ahead, would have difficulty in winning for technical reasons too involved to discuss here.

4. Ra7   h5
5. Ra5   Rd5
6. Ra3

Of course, 6. Rxd5 exd5 would be instantly fatal for White.

But after 6. Ra7, the subsequent play is not so easy: 6. . . . Kg6
7. Re7 (not 7. f5+, as Black can now reply 7. . . . Rxf5 nor
7. Kf3 Rb5   8. Ke4 Rb2   9. f5+ Kf6! arriving at a similar
position to that in the game) Rb5   8. Kf3 Rb3+   9. Kf2 h4
10. Kg2 Rb2+ 11. Kh3 Rf2 12. Kg4 f5+ 13. Kxh4 Rxf4+ and
Black, with two connected passed pawns, will win.

6. . . .	**Kg6**
7. Kf3	**Kf5**
8. h3	**h4**

An important move, as will be seen.

9. Rb3	**f6**

Now Black is able to stand a rook check without yielding
ground and can concentrate on the weak h-pawn.

10. Ra3	**Rb5**

White's rook cannot leave the rank on account of the
menace of a black rook check.

11. Rc3	**Rb2**

Threatening to win by Rh2 followed by Rxh3.

12. Rc5+	**e5**
13. fxe5	**fxe5**

Now Black has obtained a passed pawn on the e-file.

14. Rc4	

Rc8 was no better here: the scaffold is already erected.

14. . . .	**Rb3+**

15. Kg2	Rg3+
16. Kh2	

The only move to save the pawn. Now the black centre pawn is free to advance. If this pawn had been on the f-file, White could have saved the game. Black knows his endgame theory.

16. . . .	e4
17. Rc8	e3
18. Rh8	Rg6
19. Rh5+	

Not 19. Rxh4 e2 winning, nor 19. Re8 Kf4 20. Rf8+ Ke4 21. Re8+ Kd3 22. Rd8+ Ke2 and the pawn will eventually promote.

19. . . .	Rg5
20. Rh8	Kf4

20. . . . e2 would be a grave error, on account of Re8 winning the pawn and forcing the draw.

21. Rxh4+	Kf3
22. Rh8	e2
23. Re8	

Not 23. Rf8+ Ke4! 24. Re8+ Re5.

23. . . .	Rg2+
24. Kh1	Rf2
25. Rf8+	Kg3
26. Resigns	

There is nothing to be done as the white rook must keep checking because of Black's impending Rf1+ followed by e1Q. Now the black king comes back until the checks are exhausted. For example, 26. Rg8+ Kh4   27. Rh8+ Kg5 28. Rg8+ Kh6   29. Rh8+ (Rg1 is still met by Rf1) Kg7 and White's rearguard action is over. An instructive, if difficult ending.

Conclusion

A favourite query of the average chess player is: how can I improve my play? It is a question the reader will be asking sooner or later. The answer is simple – study the end game. Practice will not make perfect, but it will go a long way towards perfection – and in the ending the stakes are high!

A few test positions are given. In problems of this nature the phrase "to win" does not mean that analysis of play right up to the final mate is necessarily required, but only up to the point where victory is solely a matter of time. None of the examples is long, but each contains a "twist" that may occur in practical play. Solutions are given on page 186.

DIAGRAM 86

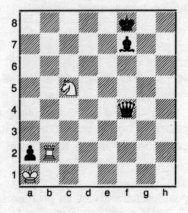

WHITE TO PLAY AND DRAW

DIAGRAM 87

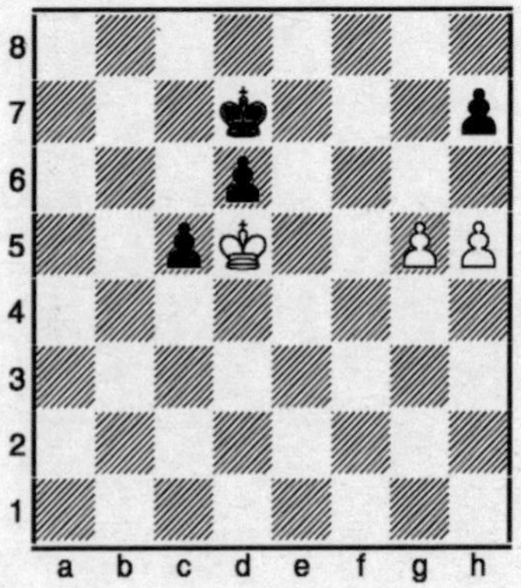

WHITE TO PLAY AND WIN

DIAGRAM 88

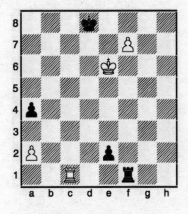

WHITE TO PLAY AND WIN

DIAGRAM 89

WHITE TO PLAY AND WIN

DIAGRAM 90

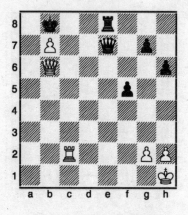

WHITE TO PLAY AND WIN

DIAGRAM 91

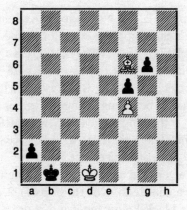

WHITE TO PLAY AND WIN

Solutions

(86) 1. Ne6+ Bxe6 2. Rf2 Qf7 (Qxf2 is stalemate) 3. Rxf7+ Kxf7 and Black cannot win (see bishop in the end game, page 73).

(87) 1. g6 hxg6 2. h6! Not 2. hxg6 Ke7 and Black wins. But 1. h6 (threatening g6) also wins for White.

(88) 1. Re1! Rf2 (if 1. . . . Rxe1 2. f8Q+ Kc7 3. Qc5+ Kd8 4. Qa5+ winning the rook, or 3. . . . Kb7/8 4. Qb4+ also winning the rook) 2. a3! (now Black is left without a waiting move and is said to be in zugzwang. If Rg2 or Rh2, the pawn queens; whilst, if the king moves, Ke7 wins) Rf1 3. Rxe2 Rf3 (the rook cannot leave the file) 4. Rd2+ Kc8 5. Rd5 Kc7 6. Rf5 Re3+ 7. Kf6 and queens next move.

(89) This is a very old ending. White, though a pawn down, is able to force a win. 1. a6! Kb8 (to stop c7) 2. Kg1! (the only move; now the black king cannot move or one of the white pawns will queen, so a pawn is compelled to advance) f3 3. Kf2 (White's strategy is to move the king in front of whichever pawn advances) h3   4. Kg3 (now Black is in zugzwang; the pawns must be surrendered in turn after which the king must move to let by a white pawn) h2 5. Kxh2 f2 6. Kg2 g3 7. Kf1 g2+ 8. Kxf2 g1Q+ 9. Kxg1 Kc7 10. a7 Kxc6 11. a8Q wins.

(90) 1. Rc8+ Rxc8 2. Qa7+! Kxa7 (if 2. . . . Kc7 3. b8Q+ and mates quickly) 3. bxc8N+ Kb7 4. Nxe7 f4 5. Nf5 and Black's pawns are decimated.

(91) 1. Ba1 (the only move) Kxa1 2. Kc2 g5 3. fxg5 f4 4. g6 f3 5. g7 f2 6. g8Q f1Q 7. Qg7+ Qf6 8. Qxf6#.

8

ILLUSTRATIVE GAMES

The six master games that comprise this chapter have been chosen to illustrate the changing styles of play over the last century and a half. They range from the swashbuckling "Immortal Game", the positional mastery of Capablanca, the genius of Fischer, the technique of Karpov and the unrivalled creativity of Kasparov to the universal style of Anand, the World Champion at the time of writing.

Game 1
This game, played in London in 1851 between two of the leading players of the day, is popularly known as the Immortal Game. Typically, both sides attack, with White sacrificing in turn both rooks, a bishop, and finally the queen.

	White Anderssen	*Black* Kieseritzky
1.	e4	e5
2.	f4	exf4

The King's Gambit. White gives up a pawn to gain time and development.

| 3. Bc4 | b5 |

Striking at the weak square f7, Black returns the pawn to deflect the bishop.

4. Bxb5	Qh4+
5. Kf1	Nf6
6. Nf3	Qh6
7. d3	Nh5
8. Nh4	c6
9. Nf5	Qg5
10. g4	Nf6
11. Rg1	cxb5

A sacrifice: the black queen now finds herself in a deal of trouble.

12. h4	Qg6
13. h5	Qg5
14. Qf3	Ng8

Black's queen finds space at the cost of delayed development.

15. Bxf4	Qf6
16. Nc3	Bc5
17. Nd5	Qxb2

This takes the queen away from the action. Sometimes called "the poisoned pawn", the b-pawn is frequently put on offer in modern opening play.

| 18. Bd6 | Bxg1 |

DIAGRAM 92

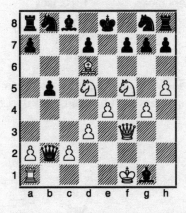

POSITION AFTER BLACK'S 18TH MOVE

The bishop moves into place for the mating net. Black now accepts the offer of the two rooks.

19. e5	Qxa1+
20. Ke2	Na6
21. Nxg7+	Kd8
22. Qf6+	

The final sacrifice.

22. . . .	Nxf6
23. Be7#	

Game 2
The strategy in this game is clear cut, White's superiority in space affording greater manoeuvrability for his pieces.

	White	Black
	Capablanca	Eliskases
1.	e4	e5
2.	Nf3	Nc6
3.	Bc4	Bc5

The Giuoco Piano is considered a slow game, as its name implies: it is much less popular than the Ruy Lopez in master play.

4. Nc3

Another good move here is c3.

| 4. | ... | Nf6 |
| 5. | d3 | d6 |

Decorous development: neither party interferes with the other – yet.

6. Bg5   h6

If Black had castled, White would have played Nd5 followed by an exchange of pieces on f6, when Black would have been compelled to recapture with the pawn, seriously compromising his king's defence.

| 7. | Bxf6 | Qxf6 |
| 8. | Nd5 | Qd8 |

To guard against Nxc7+, winning the exchange, and also of course to rescue the queen.

9. c3

White sacrificed the two bishops (marginally stronger than bishop and knight, remember) but in turn achieved quicker development. The text prepares to press home this advantage.

9. ...	Ne7
10. Ne3!	

The move presents Black with a difficult problem since on 10. ... 0-0 11. d4 exd4 12. Nxd4 White would command the centre.

10. ...	**Be6**

This move is a mistake, as Capablanca demonstrates.

11. Bxe6	**fxe6**
12. Qb3	

Threatening two pawns.

12. ...	**Qc8**
13. d4	**exd4**
14. Nxd4	**Bxd4**
15. cxd4	

DIAGRAM 93

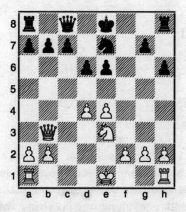

POSITION AFTER WHITE'S 15TH MOVE

The first phase may be said to be over. White, by unassuming moves, has gained a distinct advantage in the centre, a well-placed queen (against Black's passive one) and an open c-file for the white rooks.

15. . . .	**0-0**
16. 0-0	**Qd7**
17. Rac1	

If 17. Qxb7 Rfb8.

17. . . .	**Rab8**

Necessary, since White was now threatening 18. Qxb7 and if 18. . . . Rfb8 19. Qxc7.

18. Rc3	**d5**
19. Qc2	**c6**

19. . . . Nc6 would have given Black more counter-chances after 20. exd5 exd5 21. Rc5 Nxd4 22. Qd3.

20. e5	**Rf4**
21. Qd1	**Rbf8**
22. f3	**Qd8**
23. g3	**R4f7**
24. f4	**Nf5**
25. Nxf5	**Rxf5**
26. h4	

White has a pawn majority on the king's side whereas Black's queen's side majority has been rendered immobile. White controls more of the board and has a better pawn formation. Small considerations, perhaps, but enough for Capablanca to forge a win.

26. ...	g6
27. Kg2	Qe7
28. a3	

White does not wish the black queen to exercise her nuisance value on the queen's wing.

28. ...	Qg7
29. Rcf3	Qe7
30. Qc2	Kg7

Black awaits the gathering storm. White was threatening 31. g4 followed by 32. Qxg6+.

31. g4	R5f7
32. Kh3	Qd7
33. b4	Rg8
34. Rg1	Kh8
35. Qd2	

Threatening f5.

35. ...	Rh7
36. Qf2	h5
37. gxh5	Rxh5

If here 37. .... gxh5 38. Rg5, followed by a concentration of pieces on the g-file would be decisive.

38. Rg5	Qh7
39. Qg3	Qh6
40. Qg4	Rg7
41. Rg3	Kh7

On 41. .... Rh7 42. Rxh5 Qxh5 43. Qxh5 gxh5 44. Rg5

followed by f5 creating a passed pawn would give White a winning advantage.

42. Rg2

The object of this move is to bring the rook to the defence of the h-pawn and release the queen for action elsewhere.

42. ...	**Kg8**
43. Kg3	**Kh7**
44. Rh2	**Re7**

For now White did threaten Qxe6.

45. Rh3	**Kg7**

A weak move, but Black's hopes are fading. 45. . . . . Re8 was better.

46. Rxh5	**Qxh5**
47. Qxh5	**gxh5**
48. f5!	

The breakthrough.

48. ...	**exf5**
49. Kf4	**Re6**

If 49. . . . . Rf7 50. Rg3+ Kh6 51. Rg5.

50. Kxf5	**Rg6**
51. e6!	**Rg4**
52. Ke5	**Re4+**
53. Kd6	**Rxd4**
54. Re3	**Resigns**

The pawn must go through to queen.

Game 3
This game demonstrates the folly of neglecting development and the safety of the king.

	White	Black
	Fischer	Geller
1.	e4	e5
2.	Nf3	Nc6
3.	Bb5	a6
4.	Ba4	d6
5.	0-0	Bg4
6.	h3	Bh5

The ingenious sacrifice 6. . . . h5 is quite playable: if 7. hxg4 hxg4, the knight is attacked, and, if it moves, Black will threaten mate by 8. . . . Qh4.

7.	c3	Qf6
8.	g4	

This pawn advance in front of the castled king is usually dangerous; however Fischer has calculated that Black's king's side is uncoordinated.

8.	...	Bg6
9.	d4	Bxe4

White has sacrificed a pawn to open up the game.

10.	Nbd2	Bg6
11.	Bxc6+	bxc6

The black king now has no shelter on the queen's side.

| 12. dxe5 | dxe5 |
| 13. Nxe5 | Bd6 |

Not 13. . . . Qxe5 because Black would lose his queen after 14. Re1.

14. Nxg6	Qxg6
15. Re1+	Kf8
16. Nc4	h5
17. Nxd6	cxd6
18. Bf4	d5?

This move loses quickly. Somewhat better would have been 18. . . . Rd8, but Black would still have had problems developing his K-side pieces and defending his Q-side pawns.

19. Qb3	hxg4
20. Qb7!	gxh3+
21. Bg3	Rd8
22. Qb4+	Resigns

Black must lose knight and rook after 22. . . . Ne7 23. Qxe7+ Kg8 24. Qxd8+. See diagram 94.

Game 4
An example of a nicely controlled king's-side attack. The players castle on opposite sides which usually makes for an exciting contest.

	White	*Black*
	Karpov	Korchnoi
1.	e4	c5
2.	Nf3	d6

DIAGRAM 94

POSITION AFTER BLACK'S 19TH MOVE

3.	d4	cxd4
4.	Nxd4	Nf6
5.	Nc3	g6
6.	Be3	Bg7
7.	f3	

This is a sharp continuation in which White plans to castle queen's side and attack on the king's side.

7.	...	Nc6
8.	Qd2	0-0
9.	Bc4	Bd7
10.	h4	Rc8
11.	Bb3	Ne5
12.	0-0-0	Nc4
13.	Bxc4	Rxc4
14.	h5	Nxh5

White has given up a pawn to clear the file for the king's rook.

15. g4	Nf6
16. Nde2	Qa5
17. Bh6	

This is a favourite manoeuvre to get rid of a fianchettoed bishop which here both defends the king and indirectly attacks White's castled position.

17. . . .	Bxh6
18. Qxh6	Rfc8
19. Rd3	

It is necessary to defend the knight and consolidate the defence before launching the final attack on the king's side. Notice the black knight is tied to the defence of the h-pawn which is under pressure from the white queen and rook.

19. . . .	R4c5
20. g5	Rxg5

The black rook has been lured from its attacking position on the c-file.

21. Rd5	Rxd5
22. Nxd5	Re8
23. Nef4	Bc6
24. e5!	Bxd5

If 24. . . . dxe5 25. Nxf6+ exf6 26. Nh5.

25. exf6	exf6

DIAGRAM 95

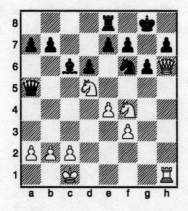

POSITION AFTER BLACK'S 23RD MOVE

26. Qxh7+	Kf8
27. Qh8+	Resigns

After 27. . . . Ke7 28. Nxd5+ Qxd5 29. Re1+ and White wins a rook or a queen for a rook.

Game 5
In this game the centre is locked, both sides castle king's side and seek play on opposite wings. This time it is Black who attacks on the king's side, and Kasparov finishes the game with a startling coup-de-grace.

White	*Black*
Piket	Kasparov
1. d4	Nf6
2. Nf3	g6

3. c4	Bg7

The "Indian" bishop is in place. White does not venture the Four Pawns' Attack (see Opening 7) and instead develops circumspectly.

4. Nc3	0-0
5. e4	d6
6. Be2	e5
7. 0-0	Nc6
8. d5	

Locking the centre.

8. ...	Ne7
9. Ne1	

In order to mobilize the f-pawn.

9. ...	Nd7
10. Be3	f5
11. f3	f4
12. Bf2	g5
13. b4	

White counter-attacks on the queen's side.

13. ...	Nf6
14. c5	Ng6
15. cxd6	

Opening the c-file.

15. ...	cxd6
16. Rc1	Rf7
17. a4	Bf8

18. a5	Bd7
19. Nb5	g4

If 20. fxg4, the white e-pawn is undefended.

20. Nc7	g3!
21. Nxa8	Nh5

Maintaining the pressure. After 21. . . . gxf2+ 22. Rxf2 Qxa8, Black gains material but the attack disappears.

22. Kh1

If 22. Bxa7 Qh4 23. h3 Bxh3 24. gxh3 Qxh3 25. Rf2 gxf2+ 26. Kxf2 Nh4 and White will have to return his extra piece, leaving Black with a winning position.

22. . . .	gxf2

DIAGRAM 96

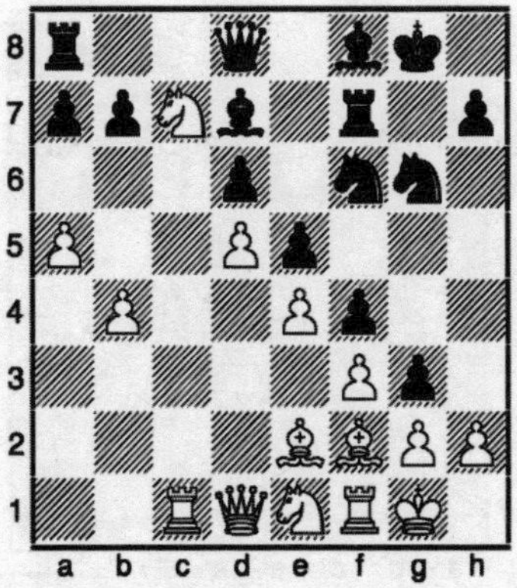

POSITION AFTER BLACK'S 20TH MOVE

23. Rxf2	Ng3+

The knight can't be taken (24. hxg3 fxg3 with Qh4+ to follow).

24. Kg1	Qxa8
25. Bc4	

White still dare not take the knight.

25. . . .	a6
26. Qd3	Qa7
27. b5	axb5
28. Bxb5	Nh1!
Resigns	

Black wins rook for knight to secure a bishop-for-pawn advantage. See final position in diagram 97.

DIAGRAM 97

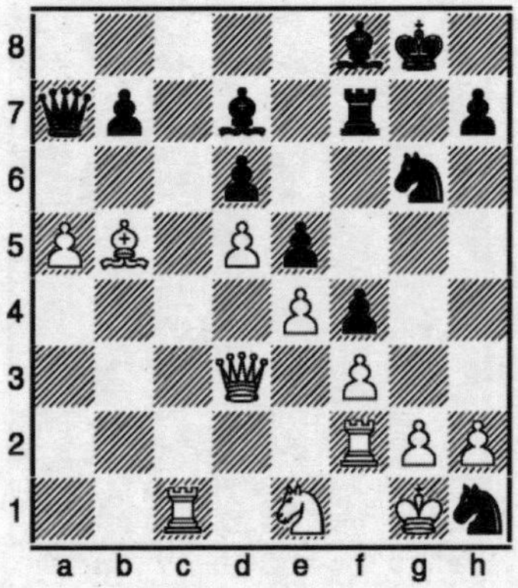

FINAL POSITION

Game 6

As chess enters the twenty-first century, players are increasingly willing to accept structural weaknesses in exchange for dynamic piece play. In this game Indian Grandmaster Anand breaks many of the accepted tenets of good play: he leaves his king in the centre while advancing his king-side pawns, at the same time sacrificing material. His exceptional judgement of the resulting position results in a swift and brilliant victory.

	White	*Black*
	Anand	Lautier
1.	e4	d5

The Scandinavian or Centre Counter Defence has become increasingly popular in recent years.

2.	exd5	Qxd5
3.	Nc3	Qa5
4.	d4	Nf6
5.	Nf3	c6
6.	Bc4	Bf5
7.	Ne5	e6
8.	g4	Bg6
9.	h4	Nbd7
10.	Nxd7	Nxd7
11.	h5	Be4
12.	Rh3	Bg2
13.	Re3	Nb6
14.	Bd3	Nd5
15.	f3	

White leaves his rook to be captured, having calculated that he will eventually be able to win the bishop on g2, and having judged that the closed nature of the resulting position will favour the white bishops rather than the black

DIAGRAM 98

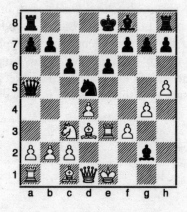

POSITION AFTER WHITE'S 15TH MOVE

rook and pawns. Black, who has reached the same conclusion, consistently refuses to take the rook.

15. . . .	Bb4
16. Kf2	Bxc3
17. bxc3	Qxc3
18. Rb1	Qxd4
19. Rxb7	

As explained in Chapter 4, rooks are at their most powerful on the seventh rank. Now Black cannot play 0-0 because he would lose his queen after Bxh7+.

19. . . .	Rd8
20. h6	gxh6
21. Bg6	

DIAGRAM 99

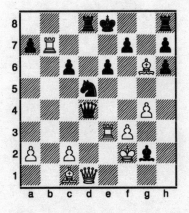

POSITION AFTER WHITE'S 21ST MOVE

An exquisite winning move. If Black captures the bishop, he loses his queen, while 21. ...Qxd1 loses to 22. Rxe6+ Kf8 23. Bxh6+ Kg8 24. Bxf7#.

21. ...	Ne7
22. Qxd4	Rxd4
23. Rd3	Rd8
24. Rxd8+	Kxd8
25. Bd3	Resigns

After 25. . . . Bh1 26. Bb2 Re8 27. Bf6, Black is in zugzwang and will soon have to lose either his knight or his bishop.

9

GENERAL INFORMATION

This short chapter, in dealing with peripherals, ignores the title and the intention of the book.

A background of general information is desirable in any game however, and this is sufficient excuse for its inclusion.

Tournament and Match Play

The first and paramount rule to remember in match play is that a chess piece once touched must be moved; and that once a piece is played (the move is completed on letting go of the piece), the move stands.

It is a very good idea to keep to this rule in friendly games; there is little more annoying than the player who dithers when making a move. Decide on your move, execute it incisively, withdraw your hand.

If an opposing chess piece is touched, the rule is that it must be captured if this is legitimately possible. If it is desired to centralize a man that has become misplaced, this can be done by saying *j'adoube* (French: "I dub") before touching the piece in question, and then only when it is your turn to move.

Matches and tournaments are decided on points – usually one point for a win, half a point for a draw.

In match play a time limit is normally imposed on the number of moves each player shall make in a prescribed period. Twenty to twenty-four moves an hour is usual, and if this time, which is allowed to each player (who is also permitted to think in the opponent's time) is exceeded, the player overstepping the time limit is ruled to have lost the game.

A chess clock is used to record the time taken by each player. In most competitions you will encounter analogue clocks but digital clocks are increasingly used in some events.

An analogue clock consists of two ordinary clocks side by side connected by a lever which, when depressed, stops the clock on the one side and restarts it on the other; hence the two clocks never run simultaneously.

When you have made your move, you press the lever thereby stopping your clock and setting your opponent's in motion. Should you omit to do this, your opponent will be thinking "free of charge".

Analogue clocks have two small strips of metal, known as flags, fixed to the dials. They are so positioned that when the minute hand approaches the hour, it will push the flag up, releasing it exactly as the hour is passed, thereby eliminating any dispute as to whether or not the time limit had been exceeded.

Digital clocks work on the same principle: they consist of two connected digital displays which show the amount of time left to each player. These devices offer alternative settings such as the increasingly popular Fischer timings, in which players receive a time increment every move.

Increasingly, time limits are set so that games are completed in one session, but many evening chess leagues still have time limits which allow the games not to be completed within the allocated time. In this case, one of two courses is normally adopted:

1. If the result cannot be agreed on the spot by the players or their captains, the game position is sent to an expert for a

decision. Adjudications of this nature are still sometimes used in team matches.

2. The game may be adjourned, the players resuming when convenient. The procedure at adjournment is for the player whose move it is to write it down without making it on the board and without disclosing it. The clocks are then stopped and the game position, together with the clock times and the sealed move (often all on the one piece of paper) are put in an envelope. The envelope is sealed and the player who made the sealed move signs across the flap. The envelope is then given to the second player to retain until the game is restarted. An illegal sealed move forfeits the game.

Players are permitted to analyse adjourned games, which they frequently do using computer software. For this reason, adjournments are gradually becoming obsolete.

Etiquette

It is not permitted in any way to disturb or distract a player during a game. In practice, this rule may prove difficult to interpret but it can be said that the player who is distracted is the best judge of what constitutes a distraction.

A player who resigns a game should obviously do so gracefully. Poor sportsmanship is unfortunately to be found in chess as it is in other games; one famous player wryly remarked that he had never won a game off a fit opponent!

Spectators should never pass audible comment on any match game in progress and nor should they interfere in any such game even if a breach of the rules has been committed.

Chess Clubs and British Chess

Chess clubs usually meet one or two evenings a week and, apart from affording the opportunity for friendly games, offer various activities such as tournaments, matches against other clubs, etc. Most chess clubs are affiliated to their respective

County Associations which in turn are affiliated to one or other of the regional Unions. These Unions, together with a few other independent bodies, send delegates to the English Chess Federation which is responsible for organized chess on a national basis.

A pleasing feature of chess life is that the traveller or holidaymaker is likely to find a welcome at the local club whether at home or abroad.

Congresses

A feature of chess since the 1970s has been the rise in popularity of the congress. A chess congress is an open tournament (usually a number of tournaments) covering anything from a day to a fortnight. Longer congresses are sometimes arranged at resorts so that the competitor combines chess with a holiday. In congresses of this nature one game is played each day, but in one-day and weekend events a fast time limit, or a time limit per game, is usual.

Chess Computers

In recent years, the chess computer has become a popular opponent. Technical development in this field has been dramatic, and software programs are now readily available that can defeat even the strongest grandmasters. A chess computer is an always-ready opponent, capable of playing at a number of different speeds and levels, and usually offering a range of other facilities including advice on the best move, retracting moves, repeating games and solving problems. All computers have built-in opening repertoires. If no human guidance is at hand, a chess computer or software program, preferably the most advanced you can afford, is a recommended purchase.

Literature

Thousands of books have been written about chess, covering the game in all its aspects. Most public libraries offer a fair selection, but average players will wish to have for their own use at least one book on the openings and one on the end game. These two books will be used mainly for reference and are essential for anyone who aspires to match or tournament play.

Two leading periodicals published in the UK are *CHESS* and the *British Chess Magazine*. There are a number of other publications as well as scores of newspaper columns devoted to the game.

Famous Players

It is invidious to attempt this subject in a few paragraphs, but some players are so widely known, if only by name, even among non-players, that these at least deserve a mention.

Capablanca and Alekhine were two former world champions (and great rivals), but it was Steinitz, an earlier champion, who probably contributed most to chess theory.

Except for the brief reign of the American, Bobby Fischer, the modern era has been dominated by players from the former Soviet Union, notably Anatoly Karpov and Garry Kasparov. In the twenty-first century top-level chess is becoming more international, with India and China the new chess powers. The World Champion at the time of writing, Vishy Anand, is Indian.

Simultaneous Chess

Simultaneous displays are a feature of many clubs' activities. A master opposes a number of players (usually around twenty) at the same time.

Each player sits at a board. The master circulates and plays a move on every board. Players withhold their replies until the master returns to their table.

Time is heavily on the side of the challengers to begin with but this advantage is gradually reduced as the number of unfinished games diminishes.

Blindfold Chess

Many strong players are able to conduct one or more games without sight of the board. Moves are announced, and the blindfold player may or may not be literally blindfolded. The world record is over forty games played simultaneously in this fashion – an incredible achievement.

Correspondence Chess

Playing chess by post or email is popular among those who have time to spare or who are inhibited by domicile or infirmity from taking part in over-the-board activities. A correspondence game may last a few months or a few years and is a good way of improving one's powers of analysis.

There are many correspondence chess organizations, both national and international, and a player may of course participate in several matches and tournaments at the same time.

Chess Puzzles

Chess puzzles which the reader is invited to solve are often published in the press. There are three main types: the game position, the endgame study and the problem. The game position is from actual play and the reader has to find the correct continuation. The endgame study is contrived, but is a position, usually a plausible game position, in which the solver is invited to demonstrate either a win or a draw. The problem is another animal: it is artificial in appearance and in its most common form requires the reader to give checkmate with White in a specific number of moves. The chess problem is an art form, designed to puzzle and entertain, not to improve one's play.

Fairy Chess

Fairy chess covers in a general sense everything which is related to but deviates from the normal game. In this sense, the games mentioned in the following section are Fairy chess. The term, however, is more commonly applied to problems. The artistic expression of the orthodox composer is severally constrained by the confines of the chessboard, the limitations of the regular chess pieces and the rules of play.

In Fairy chess, the composer makes his own conditions. These may include the use of a different board, different pieces and different rules – sometimes all three in the same problem. Some wonderful work has been done in this field.

Other Games with the Chess Pieces
There are many digressive games possible with the normal chess pieces.

Kriegspiel, Losing Game, Progressive Chess, Rifle Chess, Alice Chess – these are but a few. They are occasionally played in clubs and there is a specialist magazine, *Variant Chess*, published by the British Chess Variants Society.

Forsyth Notation
For taking down a position, the Forsyth notation is unexcelled. Facing the board from White's side, squares and pieces are enumerated, starting at the top left-hand corner (a8) and working from left to right, rank by rank. White pieces are given in capitals, black in small letters.

The position in Diagram 9 (page 29) would thus be recorded: r3k2r/ (black rook, three squares, black king, two squares, black rook) pp5p/ (black pawn, black pawn, five squares, black pawn) 1P1Bn1p1/ (one square, white pawn, one square, white bishop, black knight, one square, black pawn, one square) 2pP4/1R6/1n3P2/P2p1KPP/1R3B2.

Descriptive Notation
The principal feature of the descriptive notation is that moves are recorded from the side of the player making them, so that

each square has two descriptions, one for White, the other for Black.

The board is divided into files and ranks. Each file is named after the pieces (one on each side) that occupy it in the initial position. Thus the a-file is known as the queen's rook's (QR) file and the g-file as the king's knight's (KN) file. Ranks are numbered progressively 1–8 from the player. In the starting position, each player's king stands on K1. Moves are recorded in the same way as in the short algebraic notation except that a dash is usually inserted between the initial of the piece to be moved and the square to which it moves; also a pawn is always designated by its initial. For example, the opening moves 1. e4 e5 would be recorded in descriptive as 1. P–K4, P–K4.

Symbols are generally the same in the two systems, and ambiguities are resolved in a similar way. When capturing however, it is the piece captured that is designated, not the square on which it stands. In diagram 100 the white move R4xb3 would be written by both White and Black as R(4)xN. The descriptive equivalent of white move axb3 would be RPxN or PxN(N3); PxN would not do, because it would not be clear which knight was captured. Where confusion cannot arise, the move can be abbreviated. The white move Bg3 is described simply as B–N3 – it is not necessary to say which bishop or which N3 square because only one is possible in each case.

The system is more cumbersome than the algebraic but has the merit of being linked to the starting position whereas the algebraic is abstract.

International Chess

The Fédération Internationale des Échecs (FIDE) is the recognized world body responsible *inter alia* for the World Championship and Chess Olympiad arrangements. FIDE has ruled that the algebraic notation must be used in all official events. Nearly all countries where chess is organized are members of FIDE.

DIAGRAM 100

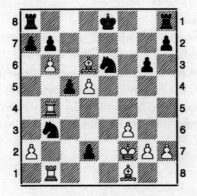

CHESS NOTATION

Master Titles

Grandmaster, International Master and FIDE Master titles for both men and women are conferred by FIDE from time to time on players whose performance in international events reached the required standard. Titles below this level (e.g. National Master, Candidate Master) are awarded by national chess authorities and vary from country to country. Only very strong players ever achieve recognition in this way.

Grading

Most countries grade players who compete regularly in approved tournaments and matches.

A player's rating, or grading as it is called in England, is derived from the aggregate of results over a period, the strength of the opponents being taken into account.

Gradings are used to determine qualification for national titles and, more widely, to assist in selection of players for matches and tournaments. They are also an incentive to the individual.

Other Notations

There are international codes for use in correspondence, radio, cable and telephone matches. Two letters or figures denote each square on the board, and a move is transmitted as a four-symbol group, the first two symbols indicating the square on which the piece to be moved stands, the second two symbols the square to which it is to be moved. Checks and captures are not annotated.

10

TEACHING YOUR CHILDREN

Richard James

During the past thirty years or so chess has become increasingly popular with young children, especially within primary schools. The purpose of this chapter is to help you help your children play better, enjoy chess more, and derive more benefit from the game.

Why?

Studies carried out in many countries have repeatedly shown that studying chess leads to improvement in children's educational attainment in both Maths and English.

Chess also helps children develop:

- Concentration
- Self-discipline
- Logical thought
- Planning
- Calculation
- Eye-brain co-ordination
- Visualization
- Thinking ahead
- Considering alternatives

- Concrete analysis
- Abstract thought
- Long-range planning
- Reading skills
- Self-awareness
- Responsibility for one's own actions
- Sportsmanship
- Etiquette
- Team spirit
- Self-esteem
- Self-motivation
- Research skills
- Aesthetic judgement
- Acceptance of success and failure
  . . . and much else besides.

It also provides opportunities for friendship with like-minded people (through joining clubs and playing in tournaments), an outlet for competitive urges, a heritage dating back hundreds of years and a literature unrivalled in its breadth and depth.

It is a game that is played in every country in the world, and can be enjoyed by everyone regardless of age, gender, race or religion.

Successful players have the chance to travel both nationally and internationally to take part in matches and tournaments. Chess provides tremendous intellectual stimulation as well as the opportunity to escape from the drudgery of everyday life into another world. Don't believe anyone who tells you chess is boring. It can be played at any speed from bullet (each player has one minute to complete the game) to international correspondence chess (where games can last several years). And if you haven't witnessed – or experienced – the excitement of a time scramble, with both players rushing to complete the game before they run out of time, you really haven't lived. Quite simply, chess is the greatest game in the world. You owe it to your children to give them the chance to try it out for themselves.

When?

While, in some cases, children can learn to play well at five, or even four, in most cases there is little advantage in children learning the moves before the age of six or seven. Younger children, however, can, if they are interested, learn the names of the pieces and how to set them up for the start of the game.

My observation over many years of teaching chess is that, unless they have a lot of support and help at home, most children who play chess at primary schools will enjoy chess only in the short term, and will find it difficult to make a lot of progress once they have learned the moves. The main reason for this is that to play chess well you need complex thinking skills which most children only develop at secondary school age. If you want your children to start playing competitively at an early age, and to develop a lifelong interest in the game, you should be aware that they need four attributes: i) to have a strong logical-mathematical and visual-spatial intelligence, ii) to be very mature for their age, both academically and emotionally, iii) to have extremely supportive parents (that's you) who are prepared to give up their spare time to take their children to clubs and tournaments, and iv) to have regular access to a knowledgeable adult (if you've read and understood the rest of this book, this will, at least in the short term, be you as well) with excellent teaching skills and the ability to relate to them on an empathetic level. If your children don't have all these traits (and do be honest, especially about the second), then, realistically, they will only receive short-term benefit from an early involvement in competitive chess. In principle, at any rate, they will gain more long-term benefit from starting competitive chess later.

However, there are two problems with this. Firstly, it's increasingly hard to motivate children of secondary school age to take up chess. This is partly because chess is so popular amongst younger children that the game is not considered "cool" by teenagers, and partly because there are so many alternative and more readily understood games to choose from. Secondly, the demands of the current education system mean that many secondary school age pupils have little time or energy to pursue demanding hobbies such as chess.

Another problem with starting young is that children will often get stuck at a certain point, failing to make progress, sometimes for a year or more. The reason for this is probably that they need to make a breakthrough in cognitive or study skills before moving up to the next level of chess comprehension. Naturally, but unfortunately, this can lead children, not to mention parents and teachers, to frustration which can result in their giving up the game. But, if they can work through this frustration they will often find that, once the necessary skills have been acquired, they make a sudden dramatic improvement.

Nevertheless, if your children's school has a chess club you should certainly use this as an opportunity to introduce them to chess. But please don't look on this as an excuse not to have to teach your children chess yourself, but rather as an opportunity for both of you to explore the wonderful world of chess together. School chess clubs, on their own, tend to put children off chess, but, with your help, your children will be able to excel at chess, and, beyond the extrinsic educational and social benefits, develop a life-long interest in the world's greatest game.

Who?

Chess at all levels is predominately male, even in most primary school chess clubs. Several reasons have been put forward for this. It is certainly true that many strong chess players also excel at mathematics, a subject in which males, on average, perform slightly better than females, and it seems that chess is more suited to what some would call a "typical male brain". However, this is a subject of much controversy and I would direct readers to the relevant literature. Chess is also, by its very nature, competitive, and this too might explain why the game tends to appeal to boys rather than to girls. There are other factors as well: girls in a school chess club will usually find themselves part of a very small minority, and will sometimes give up the game because of this.

Girls will often see chess as a way to socialize with friends, so getting a group of girls together who are all interested will help. There are also tournaments run specifically for girls which are popular and successful, and are a good way of bringing girls into competitive chess.

Although the vast majority of chess players are male, and there is some evidence that chess may be more suited to males than females, partly for cognitive reasons and partly because males tend on average to be more aggressive and competitive, there is no reason why girls cannot become excellent chess players. In families where chess is played regularly, girls will often outperform their brothers.

One good example of a very successful girl chess player was Elaine Saunders, who, in 1939, became British Women's Champion at the age of 13, and later married David Pritchard, the original author of this book. Their daughter also became a strong player.

Some readers will no doubt be familiar with the story of the Polgar sisters, three home-schooled Hungarian girls who set the chess world alight in the late 1980s. Judith, the youngest, reached the world's top ten, while Susan, the oldest became Women's World Champion.

So it is quite possible for girls, as well as boys, to excel at chess. It helps girls if they can see chess as something everyone plays together at home, if they are part of a group of friends who can play together, and if they can take part in competitions with other girls.

How?

One of the biggest frustrations for me as a chess teacher is children who have been taught incorrect strategy by their parents, and, when I try to put them right, argue that it's not what they have been taught at home, believing their parents rather than me.

Before you do anything else, read the rest of this book, if you haven't done so already, and learn how to put everything into practice yourself.

Some points to bear in mind:

1. Don't forget that the board must be set up with a white square in the right hand corner ("white on the right").
2. Make sure you use the correct names for the pieces: rooks not castles, and certainly not horses and prawns.
3. The hardest rule for children to learn is the *en passant* rule. It doesn't come up very often, but, when it does, it can make a very big difference to the result of the game. If you're not certain about this rule, go back to page 18 and check it out again.
4. Make sure you can differentiate between check, checkmate and stalemate, and that you are aware that stalemate is one specific type of draw, not another word for "draw".
5. Some popular misconceptions: a) you can't castle if you've been in check – NOT TRUE, but you can't castle if you've moved your king; b) when a pawn reaches the end it turns into a queen – NOT TRUE: you will usually choose a queen, but you could also choose a rook, bishop or knight; c) you cannot promote to a queen if you still have your original queen on the board – NOT TRUE: you can, in theory, have nine queens on the board! d) if you move your king where it can be taken, the game is a draw – NOT TRUE: if you do this you have to play a different move (with your king, if you can, if you're playing "touch and move").
6. Make sure you know about Scholar's Mate (page 58), which is very popular in primary school chess: what it is, how to play it, how to prevent it, along with an understanding that it's not going to work against an experienced player.

7. David Pritchard writes (on page 116) that, until you are
   sure of yourself, 1. e4 is the best opening move. I would
   add that, again until you are sure of yourself, 1. ...e5 is the
   best reply. Start off by learning the main openings starting
   1. e4 e5 2. Nf3 Nc6: the Ruy Lopez, Giuoco Piano, Two
   Knights' Defence, Scotch Game and Four Knights' Game.

One of the beauties of chess is its perfect balance between
strategy and tactics, and of course the two are closely interre-
lated. If you display superior strategy by putting your pieces
on better squares, tactical opportunities will arise automatically from the position. But at lower levels of chess, for
example in primary school chess clubs, tactics predominate.
Whereas experienced players will be able to play complete
games without losing material, games between young beginners are decided by the amount of material lost through
oversights.

To be successful at this level, children need to do three
things – and you will have to learn to do these as well.

1. Every move, look round the board and see if you can play
   a move which wins material (remember: pawn = 1 point,
   knight/bishop = 3 points, rook = 5 points, queen =
   9 points). If you can do this safely, then, other things being
   equal, you should do so.
2. Every move, look to see if your opponent is threatening to
   play a move which wins material. In particular, look at the
   piece he last moved, but remember that threats can come
   about in other ways, for instance discovered attacks. If you
   see a threat, you have to meet it, for example by moving
   the threatened piece, defending it if your target is not worth
   more than the attacking piece, blocking the attack or
   capturing the attacker.
3. When you've thought of a move, stop and make sure that
   the move you are considering does not lose material. Can
   my opponent take this piece if I move it there? Am I

moving away a defending piece and allowing my opponent to take another piece, or even mate me? For children, at least, this is much harder than the first two.

Some children, although they have no problems remembering the values of the pieces, are unable to put the concept into practice. They can tell you that a rook is worth five points and a knight is worth three points, but, when given the option of trading a knight for a rook, they refuse to do so because they don't want to lose their knight. In that case, ask them if they would swap £3 for £5, or three chocolates for five chocolates and they will soon understand. You can reinforce the values of the pieces by asking how much the piece they've just moved is worth. Children often enjoy adding up the values of the captured pieces to see who's ahead, which also helps develop their maths skills. You can also ask them, for instance, how much profit they'd make if they traded, for instance, a rook for a queen.

I teach my pupils to use a CCTV to look at the board. If you look for Checks, Captures and Threats, it will lead to Victory. This should be done every move of every game, looking at the board both from your point of view and from your opponent's point of view.

I have, sadly, come across children who have been put off chess by insensitive parents who play every game to win, never giving their children a chance. But, at the same time, playing badly and letting your children win every time can also be damaging. Knowing how to play against your children, and how to teach them most effectively, is vital if you want to maximize the benefits your children gain from chess.

The best personal tutors (and this is a very different skill from classroom teaching) are those who listen to their pupils, who give them the space and confidence to say what's on their mind, to describe what they are thinking about, and to express concern if there's something they don't understand. Use open-ended questions such as, "What moves are you considering?", "Why do you think I played that move?" and "What do you think will happen if you play that move?" to elicit replies which will help you learn how your children are thinking and move their thoughts in the right direction.

Many younger children have problems understanding abstract concepts such as check and checkmate so it's best to start with games with individual pieces.

Start with the pawns: a simple game is one in which the winner is the first to get a pawn to the other side of the board. In the rules I use, if you run out of pawns, or if you have no possible moves, you lose. You could start with just one pawn each. Who wins? Does it make any difference whether the pawns start on the same file, adjacent files or further apart? Then add more pawns: do two pawns always win against one? And, when you're playing these games, can you remember and use the *en passant* rule? This way, young children gain an understanding of the importance of having a material advantage as well as becoming fluent in moving pawns and learning skills which will come in useful much later when more complicated king and pawn endings are being studied.

Then, you can add pieces and try again. Knights and bishops are worth three points each so try out different positions in which three pawns battle against a minor piece. Is it better if the pawns are together or separated?

Once your children are old enough to understand check and checkmate you can start playing complete games. A good way of playing against young children is to give odds. Your child starts with a full complement of pieces while you have just your king and pawns, or even just your king. Explain that his/her most powerful piece is the queen, and that, as long as you're careful where you put her, using the queen in conjunction with other pieces will lead to a speedy victory. Look in particular at diagram 7 on page 23, with the white queen next to the black king. This will be how your children will most often get checkmate in these games, but there will be another

piece, usually a knight or bishop, rather than the king
supporting the white queen.

When your children have mastered winning at this level,
add another piece such as a knight to your side and play again.
Continue with this process, playing at each level until your
child is confident of winning, until you find a level at which
you'll have an even game.

When you play these games talk through them as you play.
If you like, you can explain your moves as you go along: "I'll
bring my knight out – it's good to get knights out early in the
game", or "I'm threatening your queen – which piece do you
think you should move next?" Ask questions to elicit information as to how your children decide on their moves. This sort
of verbalization is a useful skill anyway, and one which many
children find difficult to acquire.

Some children would rather play on equal terms straight
away rather than letting you give them a start. Again there are
several teaching techniques you can use to help them here.
Again, you can talk through the games with them as explained
above. When you reach an overwhelming position, turn the
board round and see if they can win from the other side.
Alternatively, give them the chance to turn the board round a
certain number of times during the game. Make the occasional
deliberate mistake to see if your children notice: if you like
you can say something like "Oh no! I've made a mistake!" to
provide a clue. Another technique is to choose inferior
strategy deliberately, such as moving your queen too often,
bringing your rooks out at the start of the game or moving
your king up the board to see if they can take advantage.

Joining a Club

Many primary schools have chess clubs which meet either at
lunchtime or after school. In most cases these clubs are run by
a teacher but, in some parts of the country, clubs may also be
run by professional chess teachers. These clubs are generally
run on the assumption that members already know how to

play chess, and may take the form of a tournament or ladder, with some instruction built in. If your children's school runs a club, teach them the moves at home first and make sure they know all the moves and, preferably, understand basic concepts such as check, checkmate and stalemate, and the values of the pieces before joining the club. The majority of school clubs encourage membership from Year 3 onwards, so the summer holidays before they move into Year 3 would be a good time to start fairly serious work on chess.

If your children's school does not have a chess club, you could encourage them to start one up. Perhaps you could even help run it yourself. Your school may well say that they have no one on the staff who plays chess. But with the advent of modern technology this need not be a barrier. My website chessKIDS academy (www.chesskids.com) offers free interactive chess lessons which can be broadcast to the school chess club via an interactive whiteboard, along with a download pack including the stationery you need to run internal tournaments.

In some areas there are also open junior chess clubs, which usually run at a slightly higher level than school clubs. If your children are doing well at school or at home it is well worth considering joining a club of this nature should you have one in your area. Information on this, as well as details of forthcoming tournaments and chess organizers and teachers in your area can be found on the English Chess Federation website (www.englishchess.org.uk).

Playing in a Tournament

If your children do well at school, they may have the chance to play in a tournament. Many schools run local heats of the UK Chess Challenge, in which the top boys and girls in each age group in each participating school qualify for county, and then national championships. Most areas also run local primary school chess tournaments which your children may be able to enter. Children would be well advised to be familiar with the procedures and etiquette of these events before taking part.

Tournaments of this nature are run by a team of arbiters whose job is to ensure that the laws of chess are strictly adhered to. Games will be played in silence throughout, apart from words related to the conduct of the game such as "check" and "do you want a draw?" Contravention of this rule will result in a warning, and, if repeated, a penalty. At higher levels, clocks will be used, but at lower levels this may not be the case. Check first and, if you've never played with a clock before, get some practice in before the tournament. Pairings are usually displayed on a large board with slots for cards with your name on, or, if computer pairings are being used, displayed on the wall. Tournaments are usually run on the Swiss system. In each round you will be paired, as far as possible, with an opponent on the same score as yourself, and, again as far as possible, you will alternate white and black.

All tournaments of this nature are strictly "touch and move". If you touch a piece with the intention of moving it you have to do so, and if you touch an opponent's piece with the intention of taking it, either with your hand or with one of your pieces, again you have to do so. However, there is no penalty for accidentally knocking a piece while reaching for another one. Try to avoid using the "*j'adoube*" rule (page 207) if at all possible to avoid misunderstandings: ensure that all your pieces are placed in the middle of their squares before the start of the game and that whenever you make a move you place the piece in the middle of the square. You CANNOT use the "*j'adoube*" rule to change your mind once you've touched a piece (although some children try to do this).

Draw offers are another regular source of disputes in junior tournaments. Strictly speaking, the only time you should offer a draw is between making your move and pressing your clock. Etiquette demands that you offer a draw because you think the position is level, NOT because you're losing and hope your opponent is foolish enough to accept. Not everyone understands this, though. Beware of opponents who, when losing, smile sweetly and offer you their hand, muttering something about a draw. If you accept their hand you've agreed to the draw and, sadly, there's nothing you can do about it. And DON'T try it yourself: it is totally unethical.

On the subject of draws, there is much ignorance at this level about the 50-move rule (page 26). Many children, and also many chess teachers, have three misapprehensions about this rule. Firstly, that it only applies if one player only has a king left: not true, although that's when it's most likely to come into play. If both players spend their first 50 moves shuffling their knights around, then a draw can be claimed. Secondly, there is no understanding that it is 50 moves without a pawn move or capture: therefore if the player with superior force is pushing a pawn up the board, you start counting again every time the pawn moves. Thirdly, many people think that it's 25 moves each, not 50 moves each. (There is some confusion about the use of the word "move" in chess. In this context a move comprises a turn by each player, not by just one player.)

You should be aware that, if you have a problem or something happens that you don't understand, you must stop the game, stop the clock (if you are using one) and call an arbiter, either by raising your hand or going to the control desk. If you go up to the arbiter after the game has been completed and say that you think your opponent was cheating, it's too late: there's no way anyone can do anything about it.

In most events of this nature, recording your moves is optional, but scoresheets are provided for those who wish to use them. If you're happy to do so, it's well worth doing. For a start, there are practical advantages. You have to record your moves in order to claim a draw under the 50 move rule or by threefold repetition, and you can also use it to prove, for instance, that your opponent's queen really was on the square on which you captured it, not, as claimed by your opponent, on an adjacent square. (Yes, I've seen children try this on many occasions.) But perhaps the most important reason for recording your moves is that you can go through your games afterwards, see where you went wrong and learn from your mistakes.

In many events, parents are not allowed in the playing area, and, in my opinion, quite rightly so. You're under pressure when you're playing anyway, and there's nothing worse than having someone hovering over your board watching your moves and waiting to criticize you after the game. Children who have won a game will probably want to tell you all about it. Different children will react to defeat in different ways. Some will want to tell you about the game anyway, but others will want to be consoled, or just left alone. I know from personal experience it's very difficult, but, even if you've just seen your child throw away a completely won game, try not to be overcritical. Most of us try our best when we play chess, and, because we're only human and because chess is a very difficult game, we often make mistakes. We already know when we've done something stupid and the last thing we need is someone bigger and louder shouting at us.

Chess etiquette demands that you shake hands with your opponent at the start of the game. It's a good idea to introduce yourself and wish your opponent good luck before the game begins. After the game you should again shake hands, set the pieces up for the next game, if you're using a clock and know how to do so, reset it, and report the result. The procedure for reporting results varies. In some events you will need to go up to the arbiter and report the result, while in other events you will have to fill in a result slip with the names of the players and the result of the game. It is the responsibility of the winner to report the result: the loser could falsify this, and, yes, this is something I've seen happen from time to time. Again, it's a good idea to say something like, "Well played!" to your opponent if you lost, or, "Good game" if you won. Of course children (and indeed all participants in chess competitions) should learn to accept both victory and defeat with good grace, not gloating if they win nor showing too much emotion if they lose.

Private Tuition

There is an increasing demand for private tuition for young chess players. Is this something you should consider for your children? Chess tutors may range from local enthusiasts who would charge what you would expect from a private tutor in an academic subject through to International Masters and Grandmasters who might charge many times that, but would be mostly interested in teaching at a high level to highly motivated pupils. I wouldn't recommend a private tutor for beginners: in the early stages you will be your child's best teacher and the material elsewhere in this book will give you enough knowledge of the game to do this. Do be aware, also, that chess isn't for everyone and not even the best teacher in the world will make a reluctant child interested. Again, please don't use a tutor just because you don't have time yourself. But if your child is ambitious and wants to compete at a high level, a private tutor may well be worth considering.

Do be prepared to work closely with the tutor, helping him or her to get to know your child and providing the appropriate support and encouragement. Make sure you know exactly what you want out of the chess lessons. Are you expecting mainly extrinsic benefits such as improvement in cognitive skills, or are you expecting an increase in playing strength and success in competition? First of all, the tutor and the pupil should get on well and enjoy spending time together. Secondly, don't be put off by an apparent lack of progress. As mentioned above, it's very common for children who start young to reach a plateau. This is quite natural, so don't blame the tutor if this happens. Thirdly, it's better to look at long-term chess development rather than the short-termism of hiring a tutor for a few weeks to prepare your children for an important tournament.

Computers and the Internet

There are now many ways in which children can practise and study chess using computers and the Internet, although younger children should, of course, be restricted in their amount of screen time.

With regard to software for children, I would recommend the *Fritz and Chesster* series for instruction for younger beginners. You could then move onto this software's big brother, *Fritz* or similar programs which, these days, play to a very high level. More suitable for children wanting a chess playing program, though, is the *Chessmaster* series, in which users can challenge a wide variety of virtual opponents from very weak up to Grandmaster standard. There are, however, two caveats: firstly the weaker virtual opponents play very unrealistically, and, secondly, many users have reported technical problems: this is something you should check out before you buy.

There are many sites which teach chess interactively. My own site, chessKIDS academy (www.chesskids.com) includes a fully structured course, taking children from learning the moves to adult club standard, along with quizzes, games and puzzles, five computer chess opponents of varying standards, free chess books to download and print, a schools download pack to enable any school to run a successful chess club and much advice for parents and teachers.

Finally, there are many sites on which you can play human opponents, either in real time or by email. The best site for younger children to play in real time is Yahoo Kids Chess (http://kids.yahoo.com/games/game/chess) which, with no chat facilities and no registration, is totally safe for children. For stronger players, there are sites such as the Internet Chess Club (www.chessclub.com) where playing chess is just one of many services provided for members. If you prefer to play chess by email, one of the best sites is Let's Play Chess (www.letsplaychess.com).

In Conclusion

Chess is undoubtedly one of the world's greatest games, and everyone should have the opportunity to learn how to play. For most of you reading this book, chess will simply be something you play at home or with your friends, and it's none the worse for that. But beyond this there is a wonderful world of beauty and excitement, of literature, heritage and history, of friendship and competition.

Children can gain many benefits from chess. Educational benefits are often mentioned, but I would personally rate the social benefits more highly. Having said that, chess is a fiendishly difficult game to play well, and, to be perfectly honest, it's not for everyone. Because of this, it's not always easy to find the right way to approach chess for your children. If you get it right, though, they will have, at the very least, a wonderful and lifelong interest. I hope this chapter will go some way towards pointing you in the right direction.

INDEX

Also in the Right Way series

THE RIGHT WAY TO PLAY BRIDGE

If you're a social or competitive player who understands the basics of the game, Paul Mendelson can help you to:

- Streamline your bidding and focus your play
- Discover when to obstruct with bluff
- Pinpoint the best leads
- Steal the best contracts
- Think strategically under pressure
- Outwit your opponents and please your partner

The new revised edition includes an enlarged play and defence section as well as a unique quick-reference index to take you to the right bidding chart.

Paul Mendelson is the *Financial Times* bridge correspondent and bridge professional at London's Roehampton Club. The youngest-ever captain of a winning Devonshire Cup team, he claimed the National Schools' Championship in 1983 and now runs lessons, seminars, and lectures worldwide.

To order these Right Way titles please fill in the form below

No. of copies	Title	Price	Total
	The Right Way to Play Bridge	£5.99	
	Texas Hold 'Em Poker: Begin and Win	£5.99	
	The New Mahjong	£3.99	
	For P&P add £2.50 for the first book, £1 for each additional book		
	Grand Total		£

Name: _____

Address:_____

_____ Postcode: _____

Daytime Tel. No./Email _____
(in case of query)

Three ways to pay:
1. Telephone the TBS order line on 01206 255 800.
   Order lines are open Monday – Friday, 8:30am–5:30pm.
2. I enclose a cheque made payable to **TBS Ltd** for £_____
3. Please charge my ☐ Visa ☐ Mastercard ☐ Amex
   ☐ Maestro (issue no. _____)

Card number:_____

Expiry date: _____ Last three digits on back of card:_____

Signature: _____

(your signature is essential when paying by credit or debit card)

**Please return forms to Cash Sales/Direct Mail Dept.,
The Book Service, Colchester Road, Frating Green,
Colchester CO7 7DW.**

Enquiries to readers@constablerobinson.com.

Constable and Robinson Ltd (directly or via its agents)
may mail, email or phone you about promotions or products.

☐ Tick box if you do not want these from us ☐ or our subsidiaries.

**www.right-way.co.uk
www.constablerobinson.com**